INOCULATIONS: FOUR PLAYS

Darren O'Donnell

Coach House Books

second edition

Published with the assistance of the Canada Council for the Arts
and the Ontario Arts Council

CANADIAN CATALOGUING IN PUBLICATION DATA

O' Donnell, Darren, 1965–
  Inoculations: Four Plays

ISBN 1-55245-071-6

i. Title.

PS8579.D64I56 2001   C812'.6   C00-932868-8
PR9199.3036I56 2001

to my family:
Kelly, Lianne, Mike and Troy

and

to Ken Agrell-Smith

Contents

WHITE MICE

for Libby Zeleke

THE FACT OF THE MATTER is that it is almost impossible for European societies as they are to eliminate racism in a thoroughgoing way. Racism is not simply a set of attitudes and practices that they level toward us, their socially constructed 'other', but it is the very principle of self-definition of European/Western societies. It could be said that what is otherwise known as European civilization – as manifested in the realm of arts and ideas – is a sublimated, formalized or simply a practiced version of racism.

– Himani Bannerji, *Thinking Through*

ANYWHERE but in Europe it is we whites who 'smell bad'. And I would even say that we give off an odour as white as the gathering of pus in an infected wound. As iron can be heated until it turns white so it can be said that everything excessive is white … white has become the mark of extreme decomposition.

– Antonin Artaud, *The Theatre and its Double*

Characters

ROBERT is a white-furred mouse, early thirties.

DOUGLAS is a white-furred mouse, Robert's older brother, early
    thirties.

The Actors' Relationship to the Audience

A good way to think of the predicament of doing the play is to
imagine that the production team is from another galaxy and has
come to Earth to check things out. Upon arriving the team finds
these artificially constructed 'races' – not only does the 'white' race
treat everybody else like shit but they seem for the most part to
keep themselves totally deluded about the severity of the situation.
Coming to the conclusion that the white people must be mentally
retarded, the production team from another galaxy decides to help
out by putting on this small play.

Thinking that the white folks are not smart or strong enough to
handle an overt deconstruction of their identity, they decide it would
be better to use the metaphor of mice. Practically, this plays out in
many of the moments when the actors will establish contact with the
audience, explaining finer points and often lecturing to the point of
being patronizing – but just to that point and not beyond. White
people, by virtue of a buffer born of their complicity with this state
of affairs, are amazingly stupid around this issue and must be
approached with caution.

In addition, the production team from another planet is also
aware that there will be a couple of white people and many people
of colour who are already up to speed with their understanding of
the situation, so the occasional moment can be played for them in an
obvious display of complicity.

Set

The suggestion of an apartment in downtown Toronto. The set is composed of a tiny 12' x 12' playing area, upon which are painted large cartoon-like floorboards. There is a suggestion of a back wall spanning the width of the square, created with six metal wall studs reaching high up into the grid, interrupted only by a metal arch suggesting a mouse hole. Surrounding the little area, deep behind the set, are papier mâché globes floating in the darkness; some of the globes are cut in half and placed on the ground, on the ceiling and against the walls to invoke a sense of infinity. The cartoon floor and the globes are similarly coloured to suggest that the characters float in a universe of many worlds. Set pieces include two oversized chairs and an oversized table, upon which sits a large wheel of cheese and a very large knife.

Light

The light is confined to the 12' x 12' area, with six strips of light two feet wide running up/down upstage and six running right/left, plus other specials and fills. The strips are used quickly, following the actors as they run around the small area to create a maze-like effect.

Music

The music is ubiquitous – chilled, rhythmic and soulful, and decidedly influenced by a black aesthetic, preferably composed by a black person. The ubiquity of the music and the style choice is a reference to the thorough influence of black artists in the musical world. The two mice, like most white people, always listen to music invented, inspired or created by black people.

Costumes

The costumes, while cartoon-like, are again meant to evoke the notion of white people appropriating an urban black culture – an overt hipsterism located solidly within a funky vibe yet somehow always missing the mark.

Performance Style

The two actors perform in a high-speed vaudevillian manner. Some scenes feature an overt affectation of mouseness – curled hands to indicate paws, lifted top lip to reveal mouse teeth – but other times they are human, all too human. This can turn on a dime. A definite logic is difficult, but when they are frightened or posturing they are, perhaps, especially mousy. In addition, and related to the vaudevillian style, the actors' bodies are almost always oriented straight on, facing the front or back or turned directly sideways – always avoiding any diagonal posture. Only the most tender moments between the two break this rule.

Production History

White Mice received its first reading in 1997 under the auspices of the Theatre Centre. Featuring James O'Reilly as Robert, Darren O'Donnell as Douglas, it was directed and dramaturged by Jean Yoon with additional dramaturgy by Libby Zeleke.

White Mice was first produced by Mammalian Diving Reflex in 1998, featuring Stephen Guy McGrath as Robert and Bruce Hunter as Douglas. It was directed by Darren O'Donnell and produced by Naomi Campbell, with lighting by R.A. Armstrong, music by murr, set design by Naomi Campbell and Darren O'Donnell, costumes by Samuel Jackson and Lori Hickling and stage management by J.P. Robichaud.

White Mice was presented by the World Stage Festival 2000 in association with Mammalian Diving Reflex and featured the same team, with Darren O'Donnell playing the role of Robert.

White Mice was also produced in 2000 by Theatre Passe Muraille in association with Mammalian Diving Reflex, featuring the same creative team, with SimJones Inc and Lori Hickling as the costume designers.

Overture

(The voice of a black man speaks as the house lights fade.)

HIGH IN THE TOWER, where I sit above the loud complaining of the human sea, I know many souls that toss and whirl and pass, but none there are that intrigue me more than the souls of White Folk. Of them I am singularly clairvoyant. I see in and through them. I view them from unusual points of vantage. Not as a foreigner do I come for I am native, not foreign, bone of their thought and flesh of their language. Mine is not the knowledge of the traveller or the colonial composite of dear memories, words and wonder. Nor yet is my knowledge that which servants have of masters, or mass of class, or capitalist of artisan. Rather I see these souls undressed and from the back and side. I see the working of their entrails. I know their thoughts and they know that I know. This knowledge makes them now embarrassed, now furious! They deny me my right to live and be and call me misbirth! My word is to them mere bitterness and my soul, pessimism. And yet as they preach and strut and shout and threaten, crouching as they clutch at rags of facts and fancies to hide their nakedness, they go twisting, flying by my tired eyes and I see them ever stripped – ugly, human.

– W.E.B. Du Bois

Scene 1

(Lights up to discover Douglas sitting in a chair preparing to eat the cheese and Robert standing in the doorway.)

ROBERT: I'm home.

DOUGLAS: Good, you're home.

ROBERT: Should I take out the garbage?

DOUGLAS: Do you want to take out the garbage – or –

ROBERT: Would I rather you did it?

DOUGLAS: Would you rather I did it?

ROBERT: Well –

DOUGLAS: Well what?

ROBERT: Well –

DOUGLAS: It's a simple question.

ROBERT: Frankly –

DOUGLAS: Be frank.

ROBERT: I could use the exercise.

DOUGLAS: Then go! Go! Take it out, take it out, take it out!

ROBERT: All right, here's! my! garbage! And I'm takin' it out –

DOUGLAS: On me!

ROBERT: I'm takin' it out on you, you freakin' little mouse turd.

DOUGLAS: Take it! Take it! Take it!

ROBERT: All right, I've had a fucked-up day and the same song keeps repeatin' in my head and it's all your freakin' fault!

DOUGLAS: Why's it my freakin' fault?

ROBERT: 'Cause you're my brother and I love you!

DOUGLAS: Oh, you don't.

ROBERT: Yes I do!

DOUGLAS: No you don't.

ROBERT: Yes I do!

DOUGLAS: No you don't.

ROBERT: Yes I do!

DOUGLAS: Yes you do!

ROBERT: No I don't.

DOUGLAS: See, you hate me, you stupid excuse for a stupid excuse.

ROBERT: You stupid freakin' tricker, you tricked me!

DOUGLAS: What are friends and family for?

ROBERT: What are friends and family for?

DOUGLAS: Well, since you asked –

ROBERT: Did I?

DOUGLAS: Friends and family are for fantastic fanciful folly, fraternizing, and for the further fomentation of fundamental philosophies.

ROBERT: Simply?

DOUGLAS: Friends make the world go round. Without friends we'd be –

ROBERT: Lonely, oh so lonely.

DOUGLAS: My guiding principle is to get out, meet new mice, encounter new ideas and evolve. Grow or die, that's my motto!

ROBERT: I was out today.

DOUGLAS: That's the spirit.

ROBERT: I walked for blocks and blocks.

DOUGLAS: And how did it make you feel?

ROBERT: Terrible, awful, lonely, lonely, lonely. I walk up and down the streets searching for a familiar face, a friendly smile, searching for something, anything, anything that doesn't remind me of what a stupid abysmal excuse for a stupid freakin' fuckin' freak that I am. I'm cut off!

I have no one to talk to except all the other stupid freakin' fuckin' freaks that look exactly like me, think exactly like me, walk exactly like me, and talk exactly like me! Everywhere I go I see the same stupid freakin' blank faces starin' into their own oblivion!

DOUGLAS: It's a sign of the times!

ROBERT: So ... I've decided to become political.

DOUGLAS: Political?!

ROBERT: Political.

DOUGLAS: Political?!

ROBERT: Political!

DOUGLAS: Political?!!

ROBERT: Political!!

DOUGLAS: Why?!

ROBERT: 'Cause I'm sick of this stupid freakin' fuckin' place and the way it makes me feel and I want to change it.

DOUGLAS: But! But! But!

ROBERT: But nothing! I have no hope for the status quo and if you had a soul neither would you.

DOUGLAS: But isn't your very existence political?

ROBERT: Political?! I embody the status quo. Look at me, I'm all form, form, form. I have no content.

DOUGLAS: But the content of your existence?!!!

ROBERT: It's! Not! Enough! Any more!

(Blackout)

Scene 2

(Lights up to discover Robert sitting in his chair and Douglas pacing back and forth.)

DOUGLAS: Look, what's your problem?

ROBERT: I don't know, where should I start?

DOUGLAS: I don't know. How about *(mockingly)* 'imperialism'.

ROBERT: All right, imperialism.

DOUGLAS: Take it away.

ROBERT: Well, I got a problem with it.

DOUGLAS: So join the club.

ROBERT: You don't.

DOUGLAS: Do too.

ROBERT: Do not.

DOUGLAS: Do too.

ROBERT: Do not.

DOUGLAS: Do too.

ROBERT: Do too.

DOUGLAS: Do not.

ROBERT: See! You stupid puppet of imperialist forces, you benefit from the imperial trickle-down effect.

DOUGLAS: That's been disproved. I'm one of the disposable. I'm disenfranchised.

ROBERT: Yeah, you and all your friends on College Street suckin' back the foam offa your stupid freakin' cappucciniweenies, sweating a caffeinated sheen over some stupid alien conspiracy theory, acting as if the neoconservative agenda is doing anything but creating more space for your freakin' consumption.

DOUGLAS: But I'm poor, I really am poor.

ROBERT: What's that on your whiskers?

DOUGLAS: What?

ROBERT: You heard me.

DOUGLAS: I heard you?

ROBERT: You heard me, you freakin' freak.

DOUGLAS: My whiskers are clean.

ROBERT: That's what you say.

DOUGLAS: And I'll say it again.

ROBERT: There's something white on your whiskers.

DOUGLAS: On all of them?

ROBERT: On all three of them.

DOUGLAS: I have something white on all three of my whiskers?

ROBERT: You sure do.

DOUGLAS: But, but, but –

ROBERT: It's steamed milk!! You have dried steamed milk on all three of your whiskers, so don't go telling me that your poverty is preventing a wholesale enjoyment of College Street cappuccini-weenies.

DOUGLAS: It wasn't a cappucciniweenie – !

ROBERT: Oh no?

DOUGLAS: It was a mochacciniweenie, a mochacciniweenie, for freak's sake! And I didn't pay for it, I exchanged it for some stimulating conversation with a female.

ROBERT: See! It's privilege I'm talking about, and you have it no matter how convinced of your pathetic poverty you are.

DOUGLAS: Oh sure, and the next thing you're going to tell me is that I have this holy privilege because –

ROBERT: Because –

DOUGLAS: Because –

ROBERT: Because of the colour –

DOUGLAS: – of my fur, you stupid freakin' race traitor!

ROBERT: Deny it!

DOUGLAS: Deny it?! I'm not even going to address it.

ROBERT: The hallmark of denial.

DOUGLAS: You're not going to guilt me over this one. I didn't invent this world. I didn't choose to be born. I didn't set up the freakin' rules.

ROBERT: Rules?! Oh, they're 'rules' now!

DOUGLAS: I. Am. Innocent!

ROBERT: Do you know that White mice comprise less than, do you hear me, less that fifty percent of Toronoronto's popopulation?

DOUGLAS: Big deal, what do I care? That's fine with me, I'm all for it. I like world music like everybody else.

ROBERT: Yeah, so long as you can enjoy it in a cozy supremacist atmosphere.

DOUGLAS: Supremacist?!

ROBERT: Shut your eyes!

DOUGLAS: Alrighty.

ROBERT: Picture your friends.

DOUGLAS: Alrighty.

ROBERT: Imagine a typical conversation.

DOUGLAS: Alrighty.

ROBERT: Just out of curiosity …

DOUGLAS: Yes?

ROBERT: What are you talking about?

DOUGLAS: Important things.

ROBERT: Important things?

DOUGLAS: Yeah, important things.

ROBERT: Such as –?

DOUGLAS: Well … media, films, music, careers. Careers in media, careers in film, careers in music. Careers in … careers. Interesting things. Choices. Choices that artists make. You know, politics.

ROBERT: Just out of curiosity –

DOUGLAS: Yes?

ROBERT: In this diverse city of ours with less than fifty percent of the population possessing white fur –

DOUGLAS: Yes?

ROBERT: What colour is the fur of less than fifty percent of your friends?

DOUGLAS: Well, white, of course.

ROBERT: And the more than fifty percent of your friends?

DOUGLAS: Well … *(eyes pop open)* You are a race traitor, a plain and simple race traitor!

ROBERT: And that, my brother, is fine by me!

DOUGLAS: Listen to me! Everybody's invited to come down to College Street for a cappucciniweenie. I haven't erected any fences, you stupid, arrogant, self-satisfied –

ROBERT: The problem –

DOUGLAS: Oh, here we go!

ROBERT: The problem –

DOUGLAS: You're going to tell me about the problem and –

ROBERT: The problem –

DOUGLAS: – is somehow or other –

ROBERT: The problem –

DOUGLAS: Gonna be me!

ROBERT: Why are you so freakin' fuckin' defensive?

DOUGLAS: 'Cause it's not my fault!

ROBERT: When –

DOUGLAS: It's never been my fault.

ROBERT: – did I ever say –

DOUGLAS: I love mousekind, I do, I truly do, and I just want –

ROBERT: –that it was your freakin' fault?

DOUGLAS: – everything to be okay!

ROBERT: Well, things are not okay. Okay?! Okay?!

DOUGLAS: All right, all right.

ROBERT: The problem –

DOUGLAS: Oh god, it's me, I'm the problem, I know I'm the problem.

ROBERT: – is institutional.

DOUGLAS: What are you saying?

ROBERT: And while it may be institutional, it is embodied in –

DOUGLAS: May I?

ROBERT: Dive in!

DOUGLAS: – in … the individual!

ROBERT: Take it away!

DOUGLAS: As we've learned from the various coincidences that occur just beneath the surface of one's fur, a pattern that is perceived on the macrocosm will be reflected in the microcosm which, in turn, becomes the macro for another micro and so on ad infinitum, so any system that is predicated on imbalance and inequity, such as global economics, will necessarily find itself reflected in the day-to-day adventures of even the most politically conscious mouse, so I as a straight –

ROBERT: Sorta!

DOUGLAS: – White male mouse must somehow embody all the privilege and power that is the hallmark of this stupid, horrible, lonely, lonely, lonely, sad and isolated world.

ROBERT: Exactly!

DOUGLAS: Even though –

ROBERT: What?

DOUGLAS: I have no money, my teeth are yellow from neglect, my muscles are stringy from malnutrition, my paws shake from stress, no one loves me and I love no one, and contemplating suicide is the only hobby I still enjoy.

ROBERT: C'est la vie!

DOUGLAS: And believe you me, things could be much worse. This I know, I acknowledge. I realize how lucky I am beneath all of my pathetic self-serving, self-loathing whining and complaining. Suffering is not universal and nor is it relative. I know this. I know this. I know this. And contemplating suicide is only a sublimation of my desire to get married, buy a house, and father a brood of cute furry little –

ROBERT: You're sick! You're sick! You're sick!

DOUGLAS: I'm sick!

ROBERT: Your analysis falls apart at the slightest suggestion of a freakin' breeze.

DOUGLAS: I know, I know, I know.

ROBERT: I get the distinct impression that you somehow feel that by virtue of your self-perceived saintly self-perception re your centrality, you think you truly inhabit a position of marginality vis-à-vis your location as someone in the midst of what you would not only characterize as a reversal but –

DOUGLAS: A displacement! I feel displaced!

ROBERT: And that, my brother, will be the starting point for your … Political Awakening!

DOUGLAS: Really!?

ROBERT: But remember, we mice can only learn in three. Very. Specific. Ways.

DOUGLAS: I know what you're going to say!

ROBERT: One!

DOUGLAS: By sweating!

ROBERT: Two!

DOUGLAS: By crying!

ROBERT: And –

DOUGLAS: Don't, please don't!

ROBERT: Three –

DOUGLAS: BY BLEEDING!

(Douglas grabs the knife from the table and attempts to slash his wrists. Robert grabs for the knife and a massive struggle ensues.)

ROBERT: Gimme that knife!

DOUGLAS: Don't, don't, I can't go on!

ROBERT: Give it to me!

DOUGLAS: I don't want to learn, learning is too hard!!

ROBERT: Gimme that knife, you stupid freakin' pathetic self-obsessed freak!

DOUGLAS: No, I want to die!

ROBERT: Give it to me!

DOUGLAS: I want to die!

ROBERT: You give it to me!

DOUGLAS: Please, please, please let me die!

ROBERT: No!

DOUGLAS: Let me have the knife!

ROBERT: I will not let you die!

DOUGLAS: Please, oh please!

ROBERT: You will not die!

DOUGLAS: Please!

ROBERT: You will not die!

DOUGLAS: Please, oh please!

ROBERT: You will not die!

DOUGLAS: Please let me die!

(Robert finally gets the knife away from Douglas. Douglas collapses in Robert's arms.)

ROBERT: If you ever! ever! ever! ever! kill yourself I will KILL you, do you hear me?! I will kill you!

(Blackout)

Scene 3

(Lights fade up to reveal Douglas waiting to eat the cheese. Robert stands in the entrance.)

ROBERT: I'm home!

DOUGLAS: Good, you're home.

ROBERT: How ya feelin'?

DOUGLAS: Fine, I'm oh so fine.

ROBERT: Thinkin' good thoughts?

DOUGLAS: Great thoughts!

ROBERT: Positivity?

DOUGLAS: Positively positive positivity!

ROBERT: You're on a roll!

DOUGLAS: The wind is in my sails.

ROBERT: You got it goin' on.

DOUGLAS: I'm haphaphappenin'.

ROBERT: Things. Are. Good.

DOUGLAS: Things. Are … What are you doing?

ROBERT: What?

DOUGLAS: What's goin' on?

ROBERT: What?

DOUGLAS: Why are you encouraging me?

ROBERT: I'm just trying to understand where you're coming from.

DOUGLAS: I'm not that happy.

ROBERT: Did I say there is anything wrong with happiness?

DOUGLAS: I only sound happy.

ROBERT: And you sound happy because …?

DOUGLAS: Because –

ROBERT: Because –

DOUGLAS: Well, I'm imagining a day in the distant future when I will be happy.

ROBERT: But you're not happy now?

DOUGLAS: Who me?

ROBERT: Is there anyone else in the room?

DOUGLAS: Well, you.

ROBERT: Do I sound happy?

DOUGLAS: Frankly?

ROBERT: Be frank.

DOUGLAS: No, no, Robert, you don't. You don't sound happy.

ROBERT: Don't I?

DOUGLAS: No you don't.

ROBERT: And how do I sound?

DOUGLAS: Well –

ROBERT: Do I sound sad?

DOUGLAS: No, I wouldn't call it sad.

ROBERT: How about hopeful?

DOUGLAS: It doesn't predominate.

ROBERT: Lonely?

DOUGLAS: No.

ROBERT: Confused?

DOUGLAS: Don't think so.

ROBERT: Envious.

DOUGLAS: Not really.

ROBERT: Consternated?

DOUGLAS: Constipated? How the hell would I know?!

ROBERT: Preoccupied?

DOUGLAS: No, you seem to be living in the moment.

ROBERT: Nervous?

DOUGLAS: Nope.

ROBERT: Edgy?

DOUGLAS: Close.

ROBERT: Cranky?

DOUGLAS: Maybe.

ROBERT: Content?

DOUGLAS: Ha! That's a laugh.

ROBERT: Well, how do I seem to you?

DOUGLAS: Robert.

ROBERT: Douglas.

DOUGLAS: Frankly?

ROBERT: Be frank.

DOUGLAS: You seem –

ROBERT: Yes?

DOUGLAS: Well, you seem angry, Robert, you just seem angry.

ROBERT: Do you have any idea why?

DOUGLAS: Do I have any idea why?

ROBERT: That was the question.

DOUGLAS: Robert, am I being punished for something? 'Cause if I am –

ROBERT: I'm just asking you to take a freakin' guess as to the etiology of my anger!

DOUGLAS: Well, let me see, is it some stillborn attempt at romantic contact with a female mouse?

ROBERT: What the hell do you mean by that?!!

DOUGLAS: What?! Nothing!!

ROBERT: No, what are you getting at?!

DOUGLAS: Listen, Robert, it was just a guess.

ROBERT: Just a random guess?

DOUGLAS: Listen, you freakin' idiot, I'm trying to answer your damn question.

ROBERT: Why a female?!

DOUGLAS: It's nothing! It's just been a while since you mentioned the stirrings of any sexual –

ROBERT: It has nothing, do you hear me, nothing to do with LOVE!

DOUGLAS: Who said anything about – !

ROBERT: Nothing!

DOUGLAS: All right, all right.

ROBERT: Nothing.

Douglas. All. Right. Sheesh. Is it … the weather?

ROBERT: Do you think you live encased in a tomb of propopopaganda?

DOUGLAS: So, it's not the weather.

ROBERT: Do you think the very cognitive structures that you employ on a day-to-day basis have been designed, manufactured and subtly implanted in your head, woven throughout your environment, sunken deep into your interstitial fluid, rendering your soul an automaton, proceeding automatically from directives emanating from elsewhere, guiding your every thought, your every emotion, your every action? Do you feel this way?

DOUGLAS: Well, if I did, wouldn't that very feeling be suspect?

ROBERT: Do you think that, considering the amount of mediated representation to which we are subject –

DOUGLAS: What, like TV?

ROBERT: Sure.

DOUGLAS: Radio?

ROBERT: Exactly.

DOUGLAS: Films?

ROBERT: You get the picture.

DOUGLAS: Magazines?

ROBERT: Right.

DOUGLAS: Billboards?

ROBERT: Those too.

DOUGLAS: The Internet?

ROBERT: Absolutely.

DOUGLAS: Signs that stare at you while you're peeing?

ROBERT: Especially.

DOUGLAS: Yes, of course! It's a wonder our subjectivity hasn't just dried up and vanished!

ROBERT: Exactly – it has!

DOUGLAS: It has?

ROBERT: It has.

DOUGLAS: Substantiate this outrageous claim!

ROBERT: Easy: Capapapitalism – !

DOUGLAS: Oh, for freak's sake!

ROBERT: Capapapitalism –

DOUGLAS: *(weary)* Yes, capapapitalism – ?

ROBERT: Capapapitalism has various requirements.

DOUGLAS: I'm sure it does.

ROBERT: And one of the key requirements, the key, say –

DOUGLAS: Tool?

ROBERT: – tool of –

DOUGLAS: – capapapitalism?

ROBERT: – is homogeneity.

DOUGLAS: A universalization of norms and values.

ROBERT: And therefore –

DOUGLAS: – capapapitalism –

ROBERT: – has needed to construct alliances between disparate mice to achieve certain goals.

DOUGLAS: Sounds like a good thing to me!

ROBERT: But one of capapapitalism's most substantive constructions –

DOUGLAS: Yes?!

ROBERT: Capapapitalism's most central project –

DOUGLAS: What could it be?!

ROBERT: Capapapitalism's greatest lie – !

DOUGLAS: It makes me swoon!

ROBERT: Is – !

DOUGLAS: Is?!

ROBERT: Is – !

DOUGLAS: Is?!

ROBERT: Is – !

DOUGLAS: Is?!

ROBERT: Is – !

DOUGLAS: Is?!

ROBERT: Is ... the White Race.

DOUGLAS: I gotta go! *(He quickly exits and then, just as quickly, re-enters.)* I'm home!

ROBERT: Good, you're home!

DOUGLAS: Look at my freakin' fur. Just look at it! It's WHITE! It's white, for freak's sake and no member of the freakin' fuckin' ruling class constructed me, you stupid excuse for a stupid excuse!!

ROBERT: Your Whiteness –

DOUGLAS: 'Whiteness'? It's not a quality, it's a fact.

ROBERT: – is a recent –

DOUGLAS: 'Recent'? My white fur is eternal.

ROBERT: – development.

DOUGLAS: 'Development'? It's genetic for freak's sake!

ROBERT: Your Whiteness –

DOUGLAS: My so-called Whiteness is a genetic contingency.

ROBERT: – is a historical –

DOUGLAS: 'Historical'? My race is located beyond the bounds of history.

ROBERT: – directive.

DOUGLAS: 'Directive'? From god, maybe, or my parents, or from living in frigid climes or some other such natural force that exists beyond anybody and that includes capapapapapitalism!

ROBERT: Your Whiteness –

DOUGLAS: Stop saying that!

ROBERT: – is not –

DOUGLAS: It's fate, it's plain old destiny.

ROBERT: – is not Real.

DOUGLAS: Really?

ROBERT: Really.

DOUGLAS: I am not White?

ROBERT: You are now.

DOUGLAS: But I wasn't always?

ROBERT: You, Douglas, have always been White.

DOUGLAS: You have stopped making sense and you're doing it at about a hundred miles an hour.

ROBERT: Whiteness is a club. A club to which membership has been granted over time in order to –

DOUGLAS: Let me guess.

ROBERT: Take a stab.

DOUGLAS: Divide, conquer and exploit?

ROBERT: And capapapitalism –

DOUGLAS: Oh, here we go again.

ROBERT: – constructed current racial categories –

DOUGLAS: – to divide, conquer and exploit?

ROBERT: Exactly.

DOUGLAS: So, are you telling me that, for example –

ROBERT: Irish mice –

DOUGLAS: – were not always considered White.

ROBERT: Ukranian mice –

DOUGLAS: – were not always considered White.

ROBERT: Finnish mice –

DOUGLAS: – were not always considered White.

ROBERT: Italian mice –

DOUGLAS: – were not always considered White.

ROBERT: Polish mice –

DOUGLAS: – were not always considered White.

ROBERT: And that the inclusion of these so-called nationalities, or cultures, or races, or tribes, or ethnicities, or peoples into Club White has been dependent on first –

DOUGLAS: – serving a period as cheap and expendable labour.

ROBERT: And second –

DOUGLAS: – becoming a member of a class of more-or-less propertied Canadians and thus expected to divide, conquer and exploit other mice.

ROBERT: The idea of Whiteness was first introduced in America in the 1800s in order to –

DOUGLAS: Will this be contentious?

ROBERT: Probably.

DOUGLAS: Controversial?

ROBERT: Likely.

DOUGLAS: Easily dismissed by a closed mind?

ROBERT: Absolutely.

DOUGLAS: Then lay it on me!

ROBERT: Whiteness was introduced by the ruling class to stop poor White mice from socially and politically identifying with Black and Native mice. Inventing Whiteness obscured class and forged a bogus link – the link of Whiteness – creating a White-working-class hatred toward Black and Native mice.

DOUGLAS: The White race was invented to fight socialism?!

ROBERT: Whiteness is Capapapitalism.

DOUGLAS: So, although the notion of Whiteness is upheld by consensus as operating in the Real –

ROBERT: – it truly occupies the False, and Whiteness –

DOUGLAS: – as such –

ROBERT: – and the associated psychosocial constructs proceeding from this belief in one's Whiteness –

DOUGLAS: – are strictly –

ROBERT: – delusional! A powerful tool of capapapitalist propopaganda.

DOUGLAS: So, are you saying –

ROBERT: Yes?

DOUGLAS: – that Whiteness is a dream, a trip, it doesn't exist except as a code word for global domination under the aegis of euroamericanadian capital?

ROBERT: That, my furry friend, is exactly what I'm saying.

DOUGLAS: And that my particular point of view –

ROBERT: Yes –

DOUGLAS: – my thoughts, my gaze, my – , my – , my –

ROBERT/DOUGLAS: Soul?

DOUGLAS: – is vulnerable to a monopolization process such that I, as an individual, can cease to exist –

ROBERT: As such.

DOUGLAS: As such. That my very being can blend, blur and lose its distinctive features.

ROBERT: What Capital can't assimilate and integrate it will –

DOUGLAS: Terminate.

ROBERT: – terminate.

DOUGLAS: It's like we're dead.

ROBERT: The living dead.

DOUGLAS: I find this difficult to believe.

ROBERT: Believe it.

DOUGLAS: I don't want to.

ROBERT: Of course you don't.

DOUGLAS: So I won't.

ROBERT: Don't.

DOUGLAS: Done.

(pause)

DOUGLAS: Whoops, I cut the cheese.

(Blackout)

Scene 4

(Lights up to discover the two sitting in their chairs.)

DOUGLAS: But things have always been this way. Mice have always been oppressed.

ROBERT: Picture yourself.

DOUGLAS: Alrighty.

ROBERT: Say you were a ruling member of one of the most exploitative and oppressive societies in the history of the world.

DOUGLAS: Yes?

ROBERT: Would you publicize this fact?

DOUGLAS: Of course not.

ROBERT: So, you would hide this fact.

DOUGLAS: Well, I would probably utilize all popular forms of mediation to talk up particular interpretations of history that viewed the past as being as, if not more, oppressive than the present.

ROBERT: So, you'd circulate the notion that 'things have always been this way, mice have always been oppressed'.

DOUGLAS: Circulate it?! I would freakin' fuckin'-well ensure that it was freakin' programmed into the very neural circuitry of every single commodified robot in that stupid consumerist culture, I would!

ROBERT: So, what were you saying before?

DOUGLAS: Oh, uh, I was, uh … say, what do you think's playing at the Royal?

ROBERT: Oh, probably movies.

DOUGLAS: See! Some things do stay the same!

(Blackout)

Scene 5

(Lights up to discover the two sitting casually.)

DOUGLAS: You know what I want to talk about?

ROBERT: What do you want to talk about?

DOUGLAS: Nothing. I'd like to talk about nothing.

ROBERT: You don't want to talk?

DOUGLAS: I want to talk, I want to talk about nothing.

ROBERT: Nothing?

DOUGLAS: Nothing.

ROBERT: That's very popular.

DOUGLAS: It's more interesting than you'd think.

ROBERT: You think?

DOUGLAS: To talk about something requires so much commitment, it requires an understanding of things, it requires a little effort toward formulating an analysis, and, frankly, it requires taking a position and I find that only zealots take positions; positions are not hip, they don't look good, they tend to leave you feeling like you've ruined the party, like you've said too much, like you've got snot on your face or vomit on your chin. It's about optics and positions make for bad optics.

ROBERT: Sometimes I feel lonely.

DOUGLAS: You should get a girlfriend. I'm thinking about it myself.

ROBERT: That won't necessarily help.

DOUGLAS: No?

ROBERT: No.

DOUGLAS: Aaaaaaah, nothing.

ROBERT: Nothing. I feel sick.

DOUGLAS: Sick?

ROBERT: I feel like as I get older and understand love more thoroughly the more I see how unhealthy it is.

DOUGLAS: The love of brothers, like us?

ROBERT: No, not that, I'm talking about the spectre of Romantic Love.

(He looks around as if he's seeing something.)

DOUGLAS: What is it?

ROBERT: We should paint this place.

DOUGLAS: Love and injustice, that's all I hear from you these days.

ROBERT: I talk about love?

DOUGLAS: You bring it up and then you act like you never even heard of the thing.

ROBERT: What thing?

DOUGLAS: Love!

ROBERT: Oh, that.

DOUGLAS: Yeah, that.

ROBERT: I wonder about the form that Romantic Love takes and its tendency to isolate us into these little self-consumed units of two.

DOUGLAS: It's cruel.

ROBERT: But it's a blissful cruelty.

DOUGLAS: On the carrot end of the things, maybe.

ROBERT: Yeah.

DOUGLAS: But the stick.

ROBERT: IT'S BRUTAL! BRUTAL!

DOUGLAS: Brutal.

ROBERT: What if –?

DOUGLAS: Uh huh?

ROBERT: What if the modern romantic unit –

DOUGLAS: What, the couple?

ROBERT: Yeah, that.

DOUGLAS: What about it?

ROBERT: Well, it's obviously complicit with Capitalist Hegemony.

DOUGLAS: No, it's not.

ROBERT: Yes, it is.

DOUGLAS: No, it's not.

ROBERT: Yes, it is. I don't think it's an accident that during this recent surge of capitalist triumphalism the incidence of marriage has been increasing.

DOUGLAS: Has it?

ROBERT: I love love.

DOUGLAS: But you can't hurry it.

ROBERT: No, you can't hurry love.

DOUGLAS: Is there any –

ROBERT: What?

DOUGLAS: Do you have any kind of –

ROBERT: What?

DOUGLAS: Are there any female mice that tickle your whiskers?

ROBERT: No! No no. You?

DOUGLAS: Romance?

ROBERT: Well –

DOUGLAS: Since you asked.

ROBERT: Did I?

DOUGLAS: Forget about Romance. In its current form the Love Drive is, in my opinion, inextricably linked to a way of life that is clearly not helping the lot of mousekind one bit.

ROBERT: You think?

DOUGLAS: I know. I watch.

ROBERT: Hmm.

DOUGLAS: What are you thinking?

ROBERT: Nothing. I'm thinking about nothing.

DOUGLAS: That's what I like to hear. Nothing.

ROBERT: Nothing.

(They stare off for a bit.)

DOUGLAS: What's the sound of one hand clapping?

ROBERT: I don't know, what?

DOUGLAS: Come here and I'll show you.

(Robert approaches and Douglas slaps him across the face.)

ROBERT: Really? Let me try.

(Robert slaps Douglas.)

DOUGLAS: I feel refreshed.

(As they speak they do a small dance in a sort of slow swing style.)

ROBERT: Late capitalism –

DOUGLAS: Uh huh.

ROBERT: – has created a class of mice –

DOUGLAS: Yes?

ROBERT: – mostly White mice –

DOUGLAS: Of course.

ROBERT: – who have a particular sort of leisure time that leaves them feeling both unrelaxed and unable to actually get anything done.

DOUGLAS: Thus we've developed the ability to talk about nothing.

ROBERT: For hours.

(They stop dancing and sit.)

DOUGLAS: Capital, capital, capital.

ROBERT: Capital, property and labour.

DOUGLAS: Yessiree, those are three of my favourite things!

ROBERT: I wish we had one of those devices that turn off the lights in response to a clap.

DOUGLAS: Maybe we do.

ROBERT: I guess I've never tried.

DOUGLAS: Try.

ROBERT: All right. *(claps his hands)*

(Blackout)

Scene 6

(Lights up to discover Douglas sitting and Robert in the doorway.)

ROBERT: I'm home – !

DOUGLAS: Good, you're home –

ROBERT: – and I want to talk about –

DOUGLAS: – 'cause I want to talk about –

ROBERT: – justice.

DOUGLAS: – subjectivity.

ROBERT: Well, I want to talk about justice.

DOUGLAS: Well, I want to talk about subjectivity.

ROBERT: Is justice subjective?

DOUGLAS: Is justice subjective? Well, it shouldn't be.

ROBERT: Is race subjective?

DOUGLAS: Well, of course not. It's objective. It's it's it's … who you are … you know … either you're White or you're not White.

ROBERT: Really? So either you're a mouse of colour or …

DOUGLAS: You're a mouse of … no colour.

ROBERT: What if you have one Black parent and one White parent?

DOUGLAS: Well, you're ... probably Black.

ROBERT: Why?

DOUGLAS: 'Cause you ... probably look Black.

ROBERT: But couldn't you also look White?

DOUGLAS: Well, you're whatever they look like!

ROBERT: To you.

DOUGLAS: To me?! To everybody!

ROBERT: Are Jewish mice mice of colour?

DOUGLAS: Well, they, uh, they're uh, no, uh, yeah, uh, kind of, I mean, uh, depends on, uh, who you ask.

ROBERT: So, there's no biological fact to the White race?

DOUGLAS: Well, it's ...

ROBERT: There is a sociological fact but no biological fact.

DOUGLAS: Well, should we really let facts get in the way of –

ROBERT: What unites Whites if it's not biology?

DOUGLAS: Not biology?

ROBERT: There are as many differences between those of the same race as there are between mice of different races. Why don't we categorize people according to the size of their feet?

DOUGLAS: Well, in the summer maybe but in the winter how are you supposed to – ?

ROBERT: What unites White mice if it's not biology?

DOUGLAS: Um, what letter does it start with?

ROBERT: P.

DOUGLAS: Oh, personality!

ROBERT: Maybe amongst those that have any.

DOUGLAS: That's not very nice!

ROBERT: Douglas.

DOUGLAS: Robert.

ROBERT: What unites the White race, the only thing that unites the White race is simply –

DOUGLAS: Yes?

ROBERT: Privilivilege.

DOUGLAS: Oh, that word triggers me something fierce!

ROBERT: Say it!

DOUGLAS: Do I have to?

ROBERT: Privilivilege.

DOUGLAS: *(stumbles over the word)* Privilivilivili –

ROBERT: Privilivilege.

DOUGLAS: *(continues to stumble)* Privilivilivili –

ROBERT: Privilivilege.

DOUGLAS: *(continues to stumble)* Privilivilivili –

ROBERT: Privilivilege.

DOUGLAS: Okay! Okay! But the experience of racism is a very subjective thing and while one mouse may experience the occasional, say, I dunno, um, say, bit of, you know, discriminatory behaviour does not mean that everybody does, especially here in, you know, you know, CANANANADA.

ROBERT: Reality is subjective?

DOUGLAS: Reality is in the eye of the beholder.

ROBERT: What, along with beauty?

DOUGLAS: Well, admittedly, there are some female mice who are universally –

ROBERT: What is with your fetish for female mice?

DOUGLAS: What the –

ROBERT: Are you gonna walk around and base your whole ideological framework on the contingent approval of universally beautiful female mice?

DOUGLAS: Well, now that you mention it.

ROBERT: I didn't mention it!

DOUGLAS: Didn't you?

ROBERT: You did.

DOUGLAS: I did?

ROBERT: You! Not me! You brought up romance.

DOUGLAS: Romance?!

ROBERT: Romance.

DOUGLAS: Romance?

ROBERT: Love.

DOUGLAS: Love!?

ROBERT: Love!

DOUGLAS: Love? I wasn't talkin' about love. I was proposing that reality is, um, subjective … or something like that.

ROBERT: You weren't talking about love and romance?

DOUGLAS: I was saying that while one mouse of colour may experience what they feel is um, say, um, racism, that, that doesn't mean that all –

ROBERT: So, the experience of romantic behaviour –

DOUGLAS: What?!

ROBERT: I mean discriminatory behaviour –

DOUGLAS: Yes?

ROBERT: – is merely interpretive?

DOUGLAS: Well, Canananada is not such a bad –

ROBERT: It's easy for some to say.

DOUGLAS: Like who?

ROBERT: The mice who don't have to deal with it every day.

DOUGLAS: Who needs to deal with it every day? It's time to focus up on the positive future and Get The Freak On With Things!!

ROBERT: A mere attitudinal shift.

DOUGLAS: A slight relocation of one's focus off the anger that is helping no one to a positivity that will grease the wheels on the machine of love.

ROBERT: Grease the wheels and drive straight off the cliff of a White supremacist subjectivity gone haywire.

DOUGLAS: Is that the implication of my suggestion?

ROBERT: When we have as a cornerstone of our judicial system the concept of impartial and objective decisions, this tendency you have toward privileging the subjective leads straight to a state of totototalitarianism.

DOUGLAS: TOTOTOTALITARIANISM?! WHAT THE FREAKIN' FUCKIN' FREAKIN' FUCKIN' FREAKIN' FUCK are you talking about?!

ROBERT: Wanna look at objectivity?

DOUGLAS: What?

ROBERT: Hey, you wanna?

DOUGLAS: Look at objectivity?

ROBERT: Objectively.

DOUGLAS: Weren't we talking about tototot –

ROBERT: And we still will be.

DOUGLAS: What a relief, I just love talking about tototot –

ROBERT: The justice system in, say, Ontariario –

DOUGLAS: Canananada?

ROBERT: Ontariario, Canananada.

DOUGLAS: Yes?

ROBERT: Is chock-full of subjectivity.

DOUGLAS: I thought we were going to talk about objectivity.

ROBERT: Let's talk about justice.

DOUGLAS: All right, talk about justice already!

ROBERT: Subjective justice.

DOUGLAS: Justice should be objective!

ROBERT: So, let's talk about objectivity.

DOUGLAS: Let's talk about nothing!!

ROBERT: The Report of the Commission on Systemic Racism in the Ontario Criminal Justice System –

DOUGLAS: The what the who?

ROBERT: – concludes that in the case of Black and White mice charged with the same offences, the White mouse is more likely to be released after a bail hearing even though a White mouse in the Ontario Judicial System is more likely than a Black mouse to have a criminal record and to have a more serious one.

DOUGLAS: What, what, what report is this?

ROBERT: Their conclusion was inescapable: some Black mice who were detained before trial would have been free if they had been White, and some White mice who were free before trial would have been jailed had they been Black.

DOUGLAS: Well, that doesn't seem fair.

ROBERT: Maybe not, but it suuuure sounds subjective.

DOUGLAS: And sentencing?

ROBERT: Funny you should ask.

DOUGLAS: I always love a good laugh.

ROBERT: The Report of the Commission on Systemic Racism in the Ontario –

DOUGLAS: Yes!?

ROBERT: – found that White mice found guilty were less likely than Black mice to be sentenced to prison even though the White mice were more likely to have a criminal record and a more serious one at that.

DOUGLAS: Well, shave my body and call me pink, that is incredible!

ROBERT: And, further, the Report of the –

DOUGLAS: But wait a second.

ROBERT: Yes?

DOUGLAS: Perhaps the bias originates from the fact that because of socioeconomic differences born of historical racism the Black mice are committing more crimes per capita and warrant this extraspecial attention. The White judiciary will help to rehabilitate the –

ROBERT: Poverty creates criminals?

DOUGLAS: Well, that's self-evident, it's commonsensensical.

ROBERT: All classes commit crime equally.

DOUGLAS: What the – !

ROBERT: In Thomas Gabor's U of T published book *Everybody Does It: Crime by the Public*, he found by drawing on studies of Canadian employers, employees, taxpayers, retailers, service suppliers, university students, youth, drug users and police officers –

DOUGLAS: Police officers!?

ROBERT: Police officers.

DOUGLAS: What did he find?!

ROBERT: All commit crime to the same degree.

DOUGLAS: So, it's just a matter of –

ROBERT: – who gets caught –

DOUGLAS: – as a factor of –

ROBERT: – differential law enforcement.

DOUGLAS: Differential law enforcement?! Do you mean the fact that some individuals based on the colour of their fur will receive a much higher degree of state scrutiny resulting in higher incarceration rates?

ROBERT: You're more likely to go to jail if you're Black than if you're White.

DOUGLAS: So, the thing uniting the White race is –

DOUGLAS/ROBERT: – privilivilege.

ROBERT: And prisons are becoming privatized.

DOUGLAS: Privatized?

ROBERT: So mice, some mice, some White mice will be able to make money from warehousing other mice.

DOUGLAS: And because Black mice are more likely to be jailed, another economic exploitation of Black mice is once again occurring right under the whiskers of our noses.

ROBERT: Welcome to the new Ontariario!

DOUGLAS: That sounds like tototot –

ROBERT: You're telling me.

DOUGLAS: – talitarianism!

ROBERT: What I said.

DOUGLAS: You're telling me.

(Blackout)

Scene 7

(Lights up to reveal Douglas sitting and Robert in the doorway.)

ROBERT: I'm home.

DOUGLAS: Good, you're home.

ROBERT: According to a recent study by Canananada Immigration –

DOUGLAS: Oh, for freak – ! Do we have to?!

ROBERT: – Toronoronto is the most racist city in the country.

DOUGLAS: You're negative, you're negative, can't you hear that? Can't you hear that in the very tones of your voice?

ROBERT: Toronoronto –

DOUGLAS: I heard you.

ROBERT: – is –

DOUGLAS: What difference does it make?

ROBERT: What difference?

DOUGLAS: How can you prove it?

ROBERT: Some Black mice –

DOUGLAS: What about 'em?

ROBERT: – sometimes –

DOUGLAS: Yes?

ROBERT: – experience –

DOUGLAS: I'm waiting.

ROBERT: – the streetcar –

DOUGLAS: We all experience the streetcar, unfortunately.

ROBERT: – driving past without picking them up.

DOUGLAS: What?

ROBERT: It's true.

DOUGLAS: OUTRAGEOUS!

ROBERT: Outrageous but true.

DOUGLAS: This happens!?

ROBERT: It happens.

DOUGLAS: What the freakin' fuck are you talkin about?

ROBERT: The streetcar.

DOUGLAS: Yes.

ROBERT: Sometimes.

DOUGLAS: Sometimes.

ROBERT: Does not stop.

DOUGLAS: For Black mice? That's too much. This information makes me very uncomfortable.

ROBERT: Is it too negative for you?

DOUGLAS: My point exactly. It's negative. It's negative for freak's sake. Why can't we focus on all the other times the streetcar stopped; wouldn't that be more positive?

ROBERT: Positive.

DOUGLAS: Positive positivity.

ROBERT: Positively positive positivity?

DOUGLAS: That's what the state ordered. It's very healthy.

ROBERT: You're in denial.

DOUGLAS: I have hope!

ROBERT: The hallmark of denial.

DOUGLAS: It's outrageous to fixate on the occasional racist act of the occasional streetcar driver. Things are tough all over.

ROBERT: You are universalizing.

DOUGLAS: I believe in the universe.

ROBERT: Picture yourself.

DOUGLAS: That's easy, I like doing that.

ROBERT: Boarding the streetcar.

DOUGLAS: The College car?

ROBERT: For example.

DOUGLAS: With a transfer in my hand!

ROBERT: Perfect. Do you believe there is a universal experience vis-à-vis the scrutiny of transfers?

DOUGLAS: *(opens eyes)* Let me get this straight.

ROBERT: Yes.

DOUGLAS: Sometimes Black mice will be subject to both heightened scrutiny and refused ridership on the streetcar based solely on the colour of their fur?

ROBERT: My point exactly.

DOUGLAS: In Toronoronto.

ROBERT: Ontariario.

DOUGLAS: Canananada.

ROBERT: Yes.

DOUGLAS: I'm going to try and forget that information as soon as I can.

ROBERT: And replace it with …?

DOUGLAS: Oh, an image of myself sucking my thumb and …

ROBERT: And?

DOUGLAS: … renting a video.

(pause)

DOUGLAS: There. Ahhhh. *(sniffs)* Do I smell popcorn?

ROBERT: *(sniffs)* No.

(Blackout)

Scene 8

(Lights up to reveal the two sitting in the same positions.)

ROBERT: The Report of the Commission on –

DOUGLAS: Get to the point.

ROBERT: – tells us that crime rates among immigrants are lower than among mice born in Canananada.

DOUGLAS: Seriously?!

ROBERT: From lesser dependence on social assistance to greater entrepreneurial intiatives, economically speaking, immigrants are actually better citizens all around.

DOUGLAS: Well, we should just fuckin' freakin' let in all immigrants and freakin' fuckin' deport all the fuckin' freaks born in this country!

ROBERT: Deport them?

DOUGLAS: Deport them!

ROBERT: To?

DOUGLAS: To the moon, Robert, to the moon!

ROBERT: To the moon!!

(Blackout)

Scene 9

(Lights up to reveal the two sitting in the same positions.)

DOUGLAS: You know, it's not unheard of for mice of colour to be racist toward White mice.

ROBERT: That's impossible.

DOUGLAS: Why!?

ROBERT: They may be prejudiced but –

DOUGLAS: Prejudiced based on the colour of my fur.

ROBERT: Prejudice is prejudice but racism can be defined as prejudice plus power.

DOUGLAS: Power?

ROBERT: State power, institutional power; the very mechanisms that create the forms through which we interact and these –

DOUGLAS: – are controlled by White mice?

ROBERT: As an example, in this city where half the citizens are not of European descent, on the city council, out of 56 councillors, I counted only six mice of colour.

DOUGLAS: Yes, yes, of course I know all that, I know all that but I'm not talking about the realm of the institutional but the realm of the, the, the, the personal, or the you know the, the, the … Okay, for example, when some musician of colour says they feel uninspired performing for a bunch of White mice, that's –

ROBERT: – that's perhaps tempered by the fact that White mice are constantly appropriating the various forms of creative expression invented by mice of colour and making a shitload of money off them.

DOUGLAS: Hmm … even the stupidest White mouse must have noticed that tendency.

ROBERT: And besides, would you want to perform for an audience of a whole lotta White mice?

(They laugh uproariously.)

DOUGLAS: *(notices the audience)* Well, uh …

ROBERT: *(notices the audience and speaks out of the side of his mouth)* Don't answer that.

(The lights start to fade but Douglas reconsiders and decides he doesn't want to be complicit with the joke. He stands up. The lights re-establish and Robert looks momentarily into the grid, surprised.)

DOUGLAS: Hang on! White mice aren't bad.

ROBERT: I never said they were.

DOUGLAS: You're hurting my feelings, you know, jokes like that. Maybe you can't do reverse racism – maybe it is just prejudice, but it still hurts. It hurts! I'm a nice guy, you know.

ROBERT: I never said you weren't.

DOUGLAS: I'm not a capapapitalist.

ROBERT: I never said you were.

DOUGLAS: 'Whiteness is capapapitalism.' I'm White! Or … something.

ROBERT: Forget that.

DOUGLAS: Forget it?

ROBERT: How about this: 'Capapapitalism is Racism.' Does that make you feel any better?

DOUGLAS: Is confused better?

ROBERT: Capapapitalism –

DOUGLAS: What, that again?

ROBERT: Shall we break it down?

DOUGLAS: Well, I guess it's either it or me.

ROBERT: Capapapitalism –

DOUGLAS: It's starting to feel like an old friend.

ROBERT: Creates very very very much wealth for very very few mice.

DOUGLAS: I've noticed that.

ROBERT: How does it do that?

DOUGLAS: Well, it's because the very wealthy work so much harder than the rest of us. I'm kidding!

ROBERT: The only way to make an obscenely enormous amount of money is to have other mice doing work for you. Right? Everybody knows that. I'm sorry if it's covering old ground that we all already know, but sometimes I'm like, you know, I forget how things are and I need to remind myself.

DOUGLAS: Tell me about it.

ROBERT: Workers all over the southern hemisphere create the profits that sustain America, Canada and Europe. These workers are, of course, not considered White. Whiteness has always been an attribute of the mice who do less of the work but get most of the profits. So Capapapitalism depends on a relationship between the northern hemisphere and the southern hemisphere that is profoundly unbalanced and –

DOUGLAS: Racist.

ROBERT: Capapapitalism is Racism. Capitalism created Whiteness. Without Whiteness there could be no Capapapitalism and without Capapapitalism there would be no need for Whiteness. Capapapitalism is Whiteness and Whiteness is Racism. It is that simple.

DOUGLAS: Simply simplicity at its most simple.

ROBERT: I'm glad you feel that way.

DOUGLAS: So what do we do?

ROBERT: Abolish Whiteness.

DOUGLAS: Oh, well, I've got the afternoon free, I'll get right on that.

(Blackout)

Scene 10

(Lights up slowly to reveal Douglas waiting to eat the cheese and Robert standing in the doorway. Robert seems a bit stunned.)

ROBERT: I'm home.

DOUGLAS: Good, you're home. Well, come on in, you do pay half the rent after all. Robert! Hey, Robert! Hello, Robert!

ROBERT: I just learned something very interesting today.

DOUGLAS: Oh boy.

ROBERT: I'm picturing the maple leaf.

DOUGLAS: Which one? The red one on the flag, the blue one on the hockey jersey, or the green one that I just smoked –

ROBERT: The flag.

DOUGLAS: The red one. I prefer the –

ROBERT: I'm picturing it.

DOUGLAS: You've mentioned. How's it going?

ROBERT: Badly.

DOUGLAS: Is it too pointy for you?

ROBERT: You know that kind of creepy, you know, kind of weird, uncomfortable kind of nausea, kind of dread, kind of repulsed kind of foreboding, kind of feeling you get when you look at a swastika?

DOUGLAS: I'm familiar with the feeling.

ROBERT: It's like that feeling.

DOUGLAS: You're getting that feeling from an innocent maple leaf, a beautiful symbol of this wonderful country of ours?

ROBERT: Ours?

DOUGLAS: Sure Canananada has some totototalitarian tendendendencies but, really, the swastika? Oh Robert, you are so dramatic.

ROBERT: Are you prepared to hear a quote?

DOUGLAS: I think I can handle a quote.

ROBERT: Are you sure?

DOUGLAS: Robert, it's a quote. Either I'll agree or I'll disagree, it's no big deal.

ROBERT: 'Neither Spain nor Britain should be models of German expansion but the Nordics of North America who ruthlessly pushed aside an inferior race to win for themselves soil and territory for the future.' Adolf Hitler.

DOUGLAS: Well, that sounds like some crazy fuckin' thing Hitler would say and I decidedly don't agree. Pushing aside an entire continent of mice to establish a solid land base upon which to develop a country is a fuckin' shitty thing to do and I'm pleased that he wasn't able to accomplish said task.

ROBERT: Unlike North Americans.

DOUGLAS: Unlike North Americans. Unlike North Americans?!

ROBERT: Hitler –

DOUGLAS: What, him again?

ROBERT: – based his program to exterminate the Jews, the Roma, the Poles, gays, lesbians and psychiatric patients on what had already occurred here in –

DOUGLAS: Not!

ROBERT: – Canananada. That was his genocidal plan, the plan that had first occurred here.

DOUGLAS: No, no, no, no! It was different, it was different. The Native Peoples were nomadic, they didn't actually view themselves as owning the land, just –

ROBERT: Based their entire existence on it?

DOUGLAS: They were nomadic and just got moved around a little.

ROBERT: The First Nations lived in natural bioregional configurations with most of their economics based on agriculture.

DOUGLAS: They weren't nomadic?

ROBERT: Sorry.

DOUGLAS: But there were so few, it wasn't like rounding up six million –

ROBERT: No, it was more like rounding up 100 million.

DOUGLAS: What the?!

ROBERT: 100 million.

DOUGLAS: 100 million?!

ROBERT: 100 million indigenous mice have been genocided since the European Invasion.

DOUGLAS: I know what was done was terrible, terrible, despicable, criminal, genocidal, genocidal, genocidal, but it is so over, it happened so long ago!!

ROBERT: The motivation for the extermination of First Nations –

DOUGLAS: The theft of land and resources?

ROBERT: – exists as much today as it did 50 years ago, 100 years ago and 500 years ago. And the genocide continues.

DOUGLAS: The genocide continues? Well, I don't think –

ROBERT: The theft continues, the coercion continues and the murder continues.

DOUGLAS: Murder is illegal!!

ROBERT: According to Amnesty International –

DOUGLAS: Uh-huh?

ROBERT: – the Mike Harris government extrajudicially executed –

DOUGLAS: Executed?!

ROBERT: Executed.

DOUGLAS: Amnesty International said that the Harris government executed someone?

ROBERT: Dudley George, a First Nations community leader and activist. He was singled out and told by the Provincial Police he was going to die and that night –

DOUGLAS: He did, they shot him!

ROBERT: This directive coming from the office of Premier Mike Harris.

DOUGLAS: And Amnesty International –

ROBERT: Along with a whole lot of other mice –

DOUGLAS: – has identified it as an execution?

ROBERT: A political assassination.

DOUGLAS: Thus continuing a five-hundred-year-old tradition –

ROBERT: – upon which the most famous human-rights violator in recent history –

DOUGLAS: – Adolf Hitler –

ROBERT: – based his genocidal program.

DOUGLAS: So the maple leaf may be relegated to the dustbin of history as just another symbol of fascist horror.

ROBERT: The only reason it hasn't yet is because the horror –

DOUGLAS: – continues –

ROBERT: – to advance.

DOUGLAS: I need to take a shower.

(Blackout)

Scene 11

(Lights up to reveal the two standing, in mid-argument.)

DOUGLAS: But it's always been this way, mice have always been oppressed.

ROBERT: Look, in the name of –

DOUGLAS: Capapapitalism, by any chance?

ROBERT: You read my mind.

DOUGLAS: Oh, please.

ROBERT: In the last century alone, more mice have been genocided, more species have been wiped out and more environmental destruction has occurred than in any other century in the history of –

DOUGLAS: Listen, you stupid! Stupid! That's because technology! Is getting! BETTER! That doesn't make any sense.

ROBERT: You read my mind.

(Blackout)

Scene 12

(Lights up to reveal Douglas sitting and Robert in the doorway.)

ROBERT: I'm home.

DOUGLAS: *(an edge to his voice)* Good, you're home.

ROBERT: Good.

DOUGLAS: Good.

ROBERT: Good.

DOUGLAS: Good.

ROBERT: Good.

DOUGLAS: Good. Because I'm home too.

ROBERT: Good.

DOUGLAS: And I will always be home.

ROBERT: Really.

DOUGLAS: Because this is my home, and it will always be my home.

ROBERT: Good for you.

DOUGLAS: And this is my fur.

ROBERT: I've noticed.

DOUGLAS: And it will always be my fur.

ROBERT: Will it.

DOUGLAS: And whether you like it or not, it will always be white.

ROBERT: Will it.

DOUGLAS: And that is your fur.

ROBERT: Is it.

DOUGLAS: And whether you like it or not, it will always be white.

ROBERT: Will it.

DOUGLAS: It will!

ROBERT: It's not about fur.

DOUGLAS: It's not about fur?

ROBERT: It's not about fur.

DOUGLAS: All you've been talking about is fur fur fur!

ROBERT: It's what's inside.

DOUGLAS: Inside?!

ROBERT: I am not White!

DOUGLAS: Listen to you!

ROBERT: I may look White. I may have thought I was White but I have never been White. I may have thought White but I'm not White and will never be White again!

DOUGLAS: You are insane. You are riddled with White guilt and you are full of hatred and you are full of contempt for your stupid pathetic self-loathing sorry-ass White self.

ROBERT: I AM NOT WHITE.

DOUGLAS: You can't just obliterate your culture.

ROBERT: What culture?

DOUGLAS: Your culture, your culture.

ROBERT: Which culture?

DOUGLAS: Our culture.

ROBERT: Which culture?

DOUGLAS: White culture.

ROBERT: White culture?

DOUGLAS: White culture.

ROBERT: Which White culture?

DOUGLAS: Our White culture.

ROBERT: There's no White culture.

DOUGLAS: I'll talk him down off this ledge in just a second. For god's sake, this is pure hatred you're spewing!

ROBERT: Name a White cultural attribute.

DOUGLAS: Uh …

ROBERT: Name one!

DOUGLAS: A White cultural attribute?

ROBERT: Just one!

DOUGLAS: Uh …

ROBERT: One!

DOUGLAS: Uh, Cheez Whiz … no, everybody eats that.

ROBERT: Do we have specific cultural dances?

DOUGLAS: Dances?

ROBERT: Specific cultural clothing?

DOUGLAS: Well –

ROBERT: Specific cultural songs?

DOUGLAS: 'Paradise by the Dashboard Light'!

ROBERT: Black mice invented rock and roll.

DOUGLAS: Damn, he always gets me on that one.

ROBERT: Well, name one!

DOUGLAS: Serial killing! Serial killing! You never hear about no Black folks going around serial killing!

ROBERT: All right, that's one.

DOUGLAS: Ohhhhhhhhh, there must be something positive.

ROBERT: Whiteness is not a culture. Whiteness has nothing to do with culture and everything to do with social position.

DOUGLAS: Fine, fine, there's no White culture. There's no White mice. We're all walking talking exploiters, pure scum of the earth.

ROBERT: You said it, not me.

DOUGLAS: But whatever you say about Whiteness and capapitalism and racism you have to admit that things are getting better! Don't you?! Don't you?! I mean, phones are getting smaller, pot is getting stronger and pepper spray … works! Children are shooting guns with greater and greater accuracy and Russia's Prime Minister is named Poutine! Poutine! If he becomes a problem, we'll just eat him!

ROBERT: His name is pronounced –

DOUGLAS: Bacteria's mutating faster, the weather's getting warmer, trees are getting greener, the sky is getting bluer and the cops have a helicopter! Mel Lastmouse is not just an anybody nobody, he's a somebody nobody, a somebody nobody who has given this great city MOOSE! MOOSE! But best of all about this freaking fuckin' fucked-up world, you have to admit that at least there is no more slavery. Do you hear me?! No more slavery, and that proves that things are getting better!

ROBERT: Douglas, that is not entirely true.

DOUGLAS: Oh, more holy wisdom from –

ROBERT: If you'd rather I –

DOUGLAS: Oh, no, no, no, please be my guest, you, the most angry and informed mouse-of-colour-wannabe this particular maze has ever seen, please flood my ears with your wisdom. I can hardly wait. I'd trade a hundred wheels of cheese and an entire spoon of peanut butter for one pearl of your Marxist wingdackery, so lay it on me … Comrade!

ROBERT: Slavery exists today as much as it ever has. The last decade has seen the greatest redistribution of wealth class-upwards in all of history. Fewer mice have most of the wealth than ever before. With six billion on this planet, over 4.7 billion live in abject poverty and the whole thing is divided along very distinct colour lines and it is no accident! Through the International Monetary Fund, the World Bank and various trade deals, the so-called First World has restructured so-called Third World economies, dismantling social safety nets, smashing unions and coercing these countries into supplying cheap raw materials. Self-sustaining regions, regions that used to grow a variety of produce, into growing monocultures to be only exported, food not even to be eaten by those who live on the land. The First World then responds to the ensuing poverty by sending aid packages, but only enough aid to maintain the region as a supplier of material for the West and not enough to re-establish self-sufficiency. These mice who were mainly rural now move to the cities where they provide an expendable labour force for all the manufacturing of consumer crap that is done, again, for the West. If you don't call having all of your land converted into potato fields for McDonald's, crippling your ability to produce your own food and forcing you to move to urban centres to supply cheap labour for industry – if you don't call that slavery then what do you call it?

DOUGLAS: What about here, here, here in this beautiful, bountiful fresh-faced, apple-cheeked, aw-shucks, sweetmeat, innocent-as-all-heck, hockey-stick-across-your-head, best-place-in-the-world-to-live, Cananananananada?

ROBERT: Well, speaking of Canananada, in this city alone there are more than 30,000 live-in caregivers brought here illegally who work in conditions characterized by an ever-decreasing degree of citizenship rights. Over 30,000! Ordinary Toronoronto moms and dads of ordinary Toronoronto neighbourhoods adopting women away from their families, paying them barely anything, denying them many rights. And as women recruited for nannies have progressed from being women from Britain, to South and Eastern Europe, the Caribbean and now Asia, their rights have steadily declined and today nannies have the fewest citizenship rights since slavery in Canada was phased out in the early 19th century. So, there may not be slavery, but, you know, what's a slave but somebody without citizenship rights who has to wipe the shit off your baby's ass?

DOUGLAS: AND IT'S ALL MY FAULT!!

ROBERT: Douglas.

DOUGLAS: NO, NO, IT'S ALL MY FAULT! I AM GUILTY!! ME! PERSONALLY!

ROBERT: Douglas.

DOUGLAS: *(runs around the room like a maniac, striking his breast, tearing his hair, hitting his head)* IT'S MY FAULT, IT'S MY FAULT! IIIIIIIIIIIIIII AAAAAAAAAAAAM TO BLAA-AAAAAAAME! *(He grabs the wheel of cheese and hoists it over his head and goes to throw it at the audience.)*

ROBERT: *(grabs the cheese)* You're gonna hurt someone, you fuckin' idiot.

DOUGLAS: You want to obliterate Whiteness?

ROBERT: Douglas.

DOUGLAS: *(tries to hand Robert the knife)* Why don't we start with me?

ROBERT: Douglas.

DOUGLAS: I'm obliterating me! I'm obliterating me!

ROBERT: Douglas.

ROBERT: You're all talk talk talk. This is what you want.

ROBERT: I'm not going to save you this time.

DOUGLAS: So you do think I should die? Is that what you think?!

ROBERT: I am not even going to answer that question.

DOUGLAS: You think that I as a White mouse should die, should not exist. You think that that will make everything better.

ROBERT: Look, I'm only telling you how it is, not what to do.

DOUGLAS: Abolish the White race?

ROBERT: Douglas.

DOUGLAS: Abolish the White race?

ROBERT: Douglas.

DOUGLAS: Abolish the White race?

ROBERT: Douglas!

DOUGLAS: How?!

ROBERT: Will you calm down!

DOUGLAS: How?!

ROBERT: Douglas.

DOUGLAS: How?! How do we abolish the White race?!

ROBERT: *(loses his marbles, grabs Douglas by the throat and almost strangles him to death)* HOW THE FUCK AM I SUPPOSED TO KNOW?! DO YOU THINK I KNOW EVERYTHING? WELL, I DON'T, I DON'T KNOW EVERYTHING! OKAY, OKAY, OKAY?!!

DOUGLAS: *(gurgles)* Okay, okay.

(Robert realizes Douglas can't breathe, is horrified by what he's done. Robert lets him go and they embrace, confused and terrified.)

ROBERT: Okay.

DOUGLAS: Okay.

ROBERT: You okay?

DOUGLAS: I'm okay.

ROBERT: Okay.

DOUGLAS: Okay.

ROBERT: 'Kay.

DOUGLAS: 'Kay.

(Blackout)

Scene 13

(Lights up to discover Robert standing in the doorway and Douglas sitting in a chair, no longer interested in the cheese. A moment passes, Robert says nothing. Douglas notices him.)

DOUGLAS: Well? Well? Well?

ROBERT: Well what?

DOUGLAS: Well what?!

ROBERT: Well what?

DOUGLAS: Well what?!

ROBERT: Well what?!!

DOUGLAS: You're home!

ROBERT: So?

DOUGLAS: So?!

ROBERT: So, what do you want me to say?

DOUGLAS: What do I want you to say?!

ROBERT: What do you want me to say?!

DOUGLAS: I, I, I'm at a loss.

ROBERT: *(begins to cry)* Exactly.

DOUGLAS: *(Confused, wondering what the hell to do. This he has never seen. He starts to sing a small song as if it will make it all go away.)* Ye de dee de dat dat da daddle daddle daddle de dat dat da.

ROBERT: WHY ARE YOU SINGING?!

DOUGLAS: WHY AM I SINGING?!

ROBERT: WHY ARE YOU SINGING?!

DOUGLAS: WHY ARE YOU CRYING?!

ROBERT: WHY AM I CRYING?!

DOUGLAS: WHY ARE YOU CRYING?!

ROBERT: WHY ARE YOU ASKING?!

DOUGLAS: WHY AM I ASKING?!

ROBERT: WHAT DOES IT MATTER!?

DOUGLAS: WHAT DOES IT MATTER?!

ROBERT: WHAT DOES IT MATTER?!

DOUGLAS: IT MATTERS!

ROBERT: WHY?!

DOUGLAS: 'CAUSE YOU DO!

ROBERT: NOT TO HER!

DOUGLAS: WHAT?!

ROBERT: You heard me.

DOUGLAS: I heard you? I heard something. I heard something, all right. I heard something outrageous.

ROBERT: Outrageously tragic.

DOUGLAS: Look, I'm going to start this all over again. When you enter you say what you always say and if, for some outrageously tragic reason, it has somehow slipped your mind, I will remind you: when you enter you say, 'I'm home!' to which I will respond, 'Good, you're home'. All right? Here we go, just like in the good old days, say yesterday for example. A one, a two, a one, two …

ROBERT: We have no home. We were born in this place but we are not of this place. WE are INTERLOPERS!

DOUGLAS: Robert, look, can we talk about something else? Anything else?

ROBERT: We are criminals! And we're never going to be anything other than criminals. It's our inheritance. It's encoded carefully into our bodies, woven amongst the nucleotides that form the genes that compose the DNA that string off into the chromosomes that inhabit the nucleus of our souls, and because of this diabolical formulation we will NEVER be, CAN never be, SHOULD never be allowed to feel LOVE.

DOUGLAS: Love?! What's love got to do, got to do with it? What's love but a second-hand –

ROBERT: SHUT UP!

DOUGLAS: This little conversation, if you can call it a conversation, is progressing in a manner that, while it is a bit interesting, leaves me feeling like there is something you're not telling me.

ROBERT: Douglas.

DOUGLAS: Robert.

ROBERT: There are a lot of things I haven't told you.

DOUGLAS: And that's fine, Robert. We're brothers. We're not lovers.

ROBERT: NOOOO! I HAVE NO LOVER!

DOUGLAS: Robert! I thought you knew that! I knew that. You haven't had a lover for three –

ROBERT: Hours.

DOUGLAS: What?

ROBERT: You heard me.

DOUGLAS: I heard you? I heard you. You said hours but you meant years. Right?

ROBERT: Wrong.

DOUGLAS: Oh, I see. You're telling me that today at five o'clock you had a lover but now that it's eight you are single.

ROBERT: Something like that.

DOUGLAS: Well, this is going in a direction I hadn't expected.

ROBERT: You and me both.

DOUGLAS: So … this lover; it was a brief burgeoning romance that was nipped in the bud, right?

ROBERT: If you call twelve months brief.

DOUGLAS: Twelve months?!

ROBERT: Twelve months. It's not much, but these days –

DOUGLAS: Wait a freakin' fuckin' second. You had a female friend for twelve months and you didn't introduce her to me, you never brought her home, we never watched TV together, we never took a stroll down College Street on a Saturday night with all the filmmakers and folks from North York. How can this be?

ROBERT: I was ashamed.

DOUGLAS: Ashamed?

ROBERT: She's a mouse of colour.

DOUGLAS: A mouse of colour?!

ROBERT: A Brown mouse.

DOUGLAS: A Brown mouse?!

ROBERT: A Brown mouse.

DOUGLAS: And you were ashamed?!

ROBERT: I was ashamed.

DOUGLAS: But, Robert, Robert, Robert, don't you see you fell into the very trap of which you have so eloquently spoken? I would have welcomed your brown-furred friend into the heart of our dysfunctional family, I would have welcomed her with open paws, I would have encouraged your union, I would have looked on approvingly as you settled down to a multicultural life, propagating a brood of adorable tiny mice; little Beige babies, with beige fur, beige eyes, leading one day to a totally harmonious world of Beige mice. I would have approved, Robert. You have totally underestimated me and I confess I am a little –

ROBERT: It wasn't her I was ashamed of.

DOUGLAS: What?

ROBERT: It was you, you freakin' fool!

DOUGLAS: Me?!

ROBERT: You.

DOUGLAS: What the – ?!

ROBERT: Can you blame me?! Can you?! You would have made all these stupid remarks and asked her all these stupid questions.

DOUGLAS: Stupid questions?

ROBERT: Like 'Where are you from?'

DOUGLAS: Well, where was she from?

ROBERT: See!

DOUGLAS: So what?!

ROBERT: You wouldn't ask that of a White mouse, you assume White mice belong here.

DOUGLAS: Where was she from?

ROBERT: See?! See?! I was justified!

DOUGLAS: I'm just curious for freak's sake!

ROBERT: She's from Calgary, Calgary, just like us!

DOUGLAS: We're not from Calgary, we're from Edmonton!

ROBERT: Alberta, whatever.

DOUGLAS: But I mean where's she *from* from.

ROBERT: Elsewhere, just like us!!

DOUGLAS: Like us?!

ROBERT: Like you, like me, like Mom and Dad, like Mom and Dad's mom and dad, or Mom and Dad's mom and dad's mom and dad.

DOUGLAS: All right!

ROBERT: Unless you're Native you're from elsewhere.

DOUGLAS: Well, you could have at least introduced us!

ROBERT: And if I had introduced you I'd have to be doing all this freakin' fuckin' damage control all over the freakin' fuckin' place because of your fuckin' racist ignorance!

DOUGLAS: Somehow, and I'm not exactly sure how, I feel there is something inherently racist in your very strategy.

ROBERT: What do you know, you STUPID. FUCKING. WHITE. MOUSE!!

DOUGLAS: So, why'd she dump you? Hello! I asked you a question. Why'd she dump you, Robert?

ROBERT: She dumped me because of my … racism.

DOUGLAS: WHAT?!

ROBERT: You heard me.

DOUGLAS: But you, you are the epitome of everything that is antiracist and enlightened and –

ROBERT: Shut up!

DOUGLAS: You see all, you cut through the lies like –

ROBERT: I made mistakes.

DOUGLAS: You made mistakes?

ROBERT: Of course I made mistakes.

DOUGLAS: What kind of mistakes?

ROBERT: Mistakes!

DOUGLAS: No, Mr. Cheese-Ass, Super-Fly, Avant-Analysis, Autre-Politico, Other-Futher-Mucker-Sucker, what kind of mistakes?!

ROBERT: Mistakes!

DOUGLAS: You feel you can dissect and reveal the ignorance, the racism, the hatred of others while maintaining a shroud of secrecy, a veil of denial, a web of occlusion around your own? How dare you!

ROBERT: But –

DOUGLAS: How dare you!

ROBERT: I –

DOUGLAS: HOW DARE YOU!

ROBERT: Well –

DOUGLAS: What?

ROBERT: It was like this: uh … we were, uh … making love.

DOUGLAS: You were making love?

ROBERT: We were making love.

DOUGLAS: Yes?

ROBERT: And, uh, I, uh, I heard a voice.

DOUGLAS: You heard a voice?

ROBERT: Well, it was like a voice.

DOUGLAS: What's like a voice?

ROBERT: A voice! A voice! I heard a voice!

DOUGLAS: A voice?

ROBERT: In my head.

DOUGLAS: In your head?!

ROBERT: Yes, in my head, in my freakin' fuckin' head! *(he strikes his head with his paws)* I heard a voice in my head.

DOUGLAS: What did it say?

ROBERT: It, uh, it, uh, it called her … a racial slur.

DOUGLAS: What?!

ROBERT: You heard me.

DOUGLAS: A voice in your head called your girlfriend with whom you were making love a racial slur?!

ROBERT: YES!

DOUGLAS: And you TOLD her?!

ROBERT: I was scared!

DOUGLAS: Whose voice was it?

ROBERT: Mine.

DOUGLAS: Holy fuck, you're fucked!

ROBERT: I know.

DOUGLAS: You're screwed!

ROBERT: I know.

DOUGLAS: You're RACIST!!

ROBERT: NO! *(grabs the knife and tries to slash his wrists)*

DOUGLAS: Gimme that knife!

ROBERT: No!

DOUGLAS: Give it to me!

ROBERT: No, I want to die!

DOUGLAS: No, you don't!

ROBERT: Yes, I do!

DOUGLAS: No, you don't!

ROBERT: Yes, I do!

DOUGLAS: Yes, you do!

ROBERT: No, I don't!

DOUGLAS: See, you don't, you don't!

ROBERT: I don't?

DOUGLAS: Give it!!

ROBERT: You can't stop me!

DOUGLAS: Give it to me!!

ROBERT: No!

DOUGLAS: Give it to me, you freakin' fuckin' –

ROBERT: No!

DOUGLAS: Give it to me!

ROBERT: You want it? Here! *(he holds the knife up to Douglas's throat)*

DOUGLAS: What the – ?

ROBERT: Shut up!

DOUGLAS: Hey, careful, that thing's got an edge!

ROBERT: Shut up!

DOUGLAS: Well, you are the Chief Executive Aggressor.

ROBERT: SHUT. UP.

DOUGLAS: Alrighty.

ROBERT: Of course I'm racist, you freakin' fuckin' freakfuck, how the freak am I supposed to not be? I try to take responsibility but my responsibility is tied, is complicit with this whole fucking mess. The horror of Whiteness, the poison of European Expansionism and Capitalist Triumphalism taints every inter-action, every breath, every kiss, every caress, every intermingling of whiskers, and it's too huge, too hellish and too hegemonic to deal with as an individual. I FUCKED UP!! So now I have to work to tear Whiteness apart at the root.

DOUGLAS: But I thought it wasn't about fur?!

ROBERT: It's all about fur now!! *(through this speech he addresses the audience, moving downstage, finally stepping offstage to step right up and into the audience, holding the knife perilously close to the patrons' noses)* I will go to Bay Street and I will go to Rosedale and I will hunt those who maintain this system. I will find them transfixed in the glare of their stock reports and I will slit their freakin' fuckin' throats and cut our their hearts. I will search throughout their abodes until I find their little children transfixed in the glare of their Playstations and I will slit their little throats and cut out their freakin' fuckin' hearts. I will douse their neighbourhoods in gasoline and I will burn them to the ground. And when I'm finished, I tell you, I will not have left standing a single! White! PERSON!! *(He lifts the blade and prepares to slice into a white audience member.)*

DOUGLAS: MOUSE!

ROBERT: Mouse? *(scurries back onto the stage)* Mouse, mouse, I meant mouse, I meant mouse!! Oh god, I meant mouse, I meant mouse, I swear. Ahh, fuck it.

DOUGLAS: Maybe if you found a cop and put a bullet through his brain you would feel a little better –

ROBERT: If I really thought it would make a difference.

DOUGLAS: Wow, you must have really loved her.

ROBERT: If I said that's an understatement, that'd be an understatement.

DOUGLAS: How's she doing?

ROBERT: Worse. Way worse.

DOUGLAS: Wait a minute –

ROBERT: What?

DOUGLAS: SO THAT's where you've been getting all this information and analysis. Your culturally constructed consciousness couldn't do it on its own and you had to appropriate it from –

ROBERT: All of it, all of it!! I ripped all of it off … from her! Okay? Okay?

DOUGLAS: Okay. Okay.

ROBERT: Now can we talk about something else?

DOUGLAS: Like what?

ROBERT: Like whatever.

DOUGLAS: Jazz?

ROBERT: Sure, jazz.

DOUGLAS: Okay, jazz.

ROBERT: Jazz.

DOUGLAS: I like Henry Rawlins.

ROBERT: Henry – ?

DOUGLAS: Rawlins.

ROBERT: Henry Rawlins.

DOUGLAS: I like 'im.

ROBERT: Yeah?

DOUGLAS: Do you?

ROBERT: Henry?

DOUGLAS: Rawlins.

ROBERT: Henry Rawlins.

DOUGLAS: Theee one and theee only.

ROBERT: Henry Rawlins.

DOUGLAS: Henry Rawlins.

ROBERT: No, you know, I find Henry Rawlins to be too boombastic.

DOUGLAS: Right, right, right, I know what you mean. I find myself gravitating toward the more acoustic stuff like, like, like –

ROBERT: Like Henry Mancini?

DOUGLAS: Yeah, or Sun Ra.

ROBERT: Sun Ra? The Arkestra?

DOUGLAS: Did I say Henry Rawlins? I mean Sonny Liston.

ROBERT: Yes! Especially the session he did in the, in the, the the, the –

DOUGLAS: Fifties?

ROBERT: Uh –

DOUGLAS: Sixties?

ROBERT: Um –

DOUGLAS: Seventies?

ROBERT: Was it?

DOUGLAS: Or maybe the, uh, what's after the seventies – ?

ROBERT: The nineties.

DOUGLAS: The nineties.

ROBERT: Yeah, yeah, yeah, the purely improvised session he did with that supersonic crack ensemble of –

DOUGLAS: The one he did with Sonny Boy Rawlins.

ROBERT: Yeah! That one!

DOUGLAS: And Miles Cherry!

ROBERT: Right!

DOUGLAS: And Don Shepp!

ROBERT: Exactly.

DOUGLAS: And Archie Davis.

ROBERT: Ah, those were the days.

DOUGLAS: And Ornette Coletrane.

ROBERT: Take me back.

DOUGLAS: And John Coleman.

ROBERT: Tuck me in.

DOUGLAS: And Thelonius Mingus.

ROBERT: Turn out the light.

DOUGLAS: And Stan Getz.

ROBERT: Don't want to forget about ol' Stan.

DOUGLAS: Not Stan.

ROBERT: Stan the Man.

ROBERT/DOUGLAS: Yup.

DOUGLAS: Things are going to be okay.

ROBERT: No, they're not.

DOUGLAS: Things are better. Mice are becoming more tolerant.

ROBERT: No, they're not. We're in the midst of a race war. Look around you – who drives all the cabs in this city, who washes all the dishes in all the restaurants, whose faces cram the courts and work the night shift at the Taco Bell, who won't landlords rent to, and who do the cops shoot when they shoot to kill? It would be embarrassing if it wasn't so terrifying. And the incredible thing is that White mice, they can't see it. It's so incredibly denied. They could listen to us talk about it for an hour and they'd believe they had understood, but the simplicity of the facts, the simplicity, for example, of the simple fact that Canada was the living embodiment of Hitler's dreams will be lost the minute they walked away. Vanished into that vacuum most White mice call their souls.

DOUGLAS: Things are not as horrible as you make them out.

ROBERT: No, they're worse. And they're going to keep on getting that way.

DOUGLAS: I know you're not going to want to hear this but I think your perception of reality is a little skewed due to the trauma of the collapse of your recent relationship. I agree that racism is a problem but I don't think it informs everything, like you claim.

ROBERT: Next time you go outside –

DOUGLAS: Yes?

ROBERT: Open your eyes and never let them blink, no matter how filled with tears they may become, you are to never blink. Your eyes will burn, oh how they will burn, but never let them blink, never let them blink even once, never blink, hold them open through the dust and the propaganda and the manipulation but never, ever, blink. Just promise me you'll do that the next time you go outside.

DOUGLAS: Can I use toothpicks?

ROBERT: You can staple them open for all I care.

DOUGLAS: All right, next time I go out I won't blink.

ROBERT: Not once.

DOUGLAS: Not once.

ROBERT: For me, for our friendship.

DOUGLAS: For our friendship.

ROBERT: And for yourself, for your soul.

DOUGLAS: For my soul.

ROBERT: Promise.

DOUGLAS: I promise.

ROBERT: You won't –

DOUGLAS: Blink.

(Blackout)

Scene 14

(Douglas stands dazed in the doorway, his eyes wide with horror and amazement while Robert sits in his chair.)

DOUGLAS: I'm home.

ROBERT: Did you blink?

DOUGLAS: I'm home.

ROBERT: You didn't blink.

DOUGLAS: It's everywhere.

ROBERT: Yup.

DOUGLAS: It's everything.

ROBERT: Yup.

DOUGLAS: It's everywhere, it's everything.

ROBERT: I thought you'd never notice.

DOUGLAS: Well, what are we going to do?

ROBERT: Do?

DOUGLAS: To stop it!

ROBERT: How the hell am I supposed to know.

DOUGLAS: Well, freak it, I need to know! The atrocities continue to escalate while I sit back idly doing nothing, spending the rest of my life locked in dead conversations with other dead White mice propagating my murderous so-called culture?

ROBERT: Yup, those are the implications.

DOUGLAS: You bring me this far and now you abandon me?! Thanks a lot!

ROBERT: I'M IN THE SAME FREAKIN' FUCKIN' BOAT AS YOU!! DON'T YOU GET IT?!

DOUGLAS: Great, just fuckin' great! My identity is not only bankrupt but predicated on genocide and every conversation I have with mice I used to consider my friends is like talking to walking corpses. Holy shit! I'm going to fucking go insane!

ROBERT: Think about something else!

DOUGLAS: How the hell am I supposed to think about something else?

ROBERT: Just do it before I do it for you!

DOUGLAS: Something else, something else, something else … hmmm … what was she like, your girlfriend, I mean your ex?

ROBERT: Anything but that.

DOUGLAS: Oh, uh, well, you learned a lot from her –

ROBERT: Will you please!

DOUGLAS: I can't think of anything else!

ROBERT: Talk about a movie!

DOUGLAS: What?

ROBERT: Talk about TV.

DOUGLAS: TV?

ROBERT: Talk about anything.

DOUGLAS: Uh, TV, TV –

ROBERT: Television.

DOUGLAS: I know what the letters stand for.

ROBERT: Talk about it.

DOUGLAS: Uh, you know the guy from *Law and Order*?

ROBERT: Which guy?

DOUGLAS: The guy, the guy, the guy who was in that other thing, that other show.

ROBERT: Which other show?

DOUGLAS: That film.

ROBERT: Which film?

DOUGLAS: The film, the film, the film that was made by that guy.

ROBERT: Which guy?

DOUGLAS: The guy who made that film based on that book.

ROBERT: Book?

DOUGLAS: The book, the book written by the female that wrote that trilogy or tetralogy or, what's five?

ROBERT: Five?

DOUGLAS: What's a series of five?

ROBERT: Of five?

DOUGLAS: Five, you know, a series of five, what's French for five?

ROBERT: Cinq.

DOUGLAS: Cinqology. No, that's not it. Anyway, the female, the female who wrote that series about that planet with those flowers.

ROBERT: The flowers with the singing stamens?

DOUGLAS: Pistils, they had singing pistils.

ROBERT: They were stamens, the pistil is the part of the plant that has the powdery stuff on it.

DOUGLAS: Cocaine?

ROBERT: No, not cocaine, you idiot.

DOUGLAS: Do you feel better now?

ROBERT: Better?

DOUGLAS: Have you forgotten about ... all of it?

ROBERT: What about the guy from *Law and Order*?

DOUGLAS: Oh, uh, um ...

ROBERT: Tell me about the people on TV! Please tell me, how are they doing?!

DOUGLAS: What?

ROBERT: How are the television people?

DOUGLAS: Uh, I think you're becoming nuts.

ROBERT: I'm nuts?

DOUGLAS: It's just a guess.

ROBERT: I'm getting out of this fucking place.

DOUGLAS: Yeah, where are you going to go?

ROBERT: There's gotta be a way to get a message out of here.

DOUGLAS: Out of where?

ROBERT: Here! Here! Here!

DOUGLAS: You are nuts! Here is everywhere!

ROBERT: There's got to be a way!

DOUGLAS: Are you talking about travelling?

ROBERT: Yeah, travel.

DOUGLAS: You're not going anywhere.

ROBERT: I'm hoping for a ticket out of this place.

DOUGLAS: What the hell are you talking about?

ROBERT: I'm talkin' about the slightest chance that maybe just perhaps whatever it was that got us here – the spaceship that crashed that was carrying the First Mice, just perhaps, the place from which we have come has sent out a search team, and they're looking for us and they're going to fly by and they're going to take us all home, home away from all this hatred and greed.

DOUGLAS: There's no spaceship.

ROBERT: No?

DOUGLAS: There is no intergalactic family racing to our rescue.

ROBERT: No?

DOUGLAS: There's just us, us, mice, little mice! Little mice running around a …

ROBERT: What is this place?

DOUGLAS: Don't ask! Never ask!

ROBERT: At least if I was in a trap I could chew my leg off!!

DOUGLAS: Shut up shut up shut up! Talk to me about e-mail.

ROBERT: E-mail?

DOUGLAS: Anything, anything, dot-com, dot-com, do you think the whole dot-com thing is overhyped?

ROBERT: Uh, I think Don McKellar is underrated.

DOUGLAS: Underrated?! The guy keeps winnin' freakin' fuckin' awards, people are rating him just fine.

ROBERT: Did you say something about e-mail?

DOUGLAS: Who me?

ROBERT: E-mail, now e-mail, that hasn't won any awards at Cannes.

DOUGLAS: I didn't know it could.

ROBERT: It can't. *(pronounces it 'cawn't')*

DOUGLAS: It can't? *(pronounces it 'cawn't')*

ROBERT: It can't.

DOUGLAS: It can't.

ROBERT: No, not even vis-à-vis –

DOUGLAS: Hey, I get to say 'vis-à-vis' next.

ROBERT: What?

DOUGLAS: I get to say it next.

ROBERT: No you don't, I do.

DOUGLAS: No, it's my turn.

ROBERT: You already said it today.

DOUGLAS: Yeah and then you said it after.

ROBERT: I did?

DOUGLAS: Yeah, you said it vis-à-vis mutual funds, UK Garage and road rage.

ROBERT: Oh, that's right. Well then, go ahead, say it.

DOUGLAS: Vis-à-vis.

ROBERT: How'd it feel?

DOUGLAS: Great, that felt really great …

ROBERT: Yeah?

DOUGLAS: Yeah.

ROBERT: Yeah?

DOUGLAS: Yeah.

ROBERT: Yeah.

DOUGLAS: Yeah.

ROBERT: Yeah.

DOUGLAS: Yeah, yeah I'm starting to feel better.

ROBERT: Yeah!?

DOUGLAS: I'm starting to feel like my good ol' complacent White self.

ROBERT: AHHHHH!

DOUGLAS: AHHHHHH!

ROBERT: This place is programmed to make you forget everything that's important. It's heinous!! It's heinous!!

DOUGLAS: But think – it's not supposed to be easy! This can't be easy!

ROBERT: This can't be easy?

DOUGLAS: It can't be easy.

ROBERT: It can't be easy.

DOUGLAS: It can't be easy.

ROBERT: Why can't it be easy?

DOUGLAS: This is about staying awake. This is about staying alert. We are under siege. If our lives are to be based on anything more than banal discussions of popular culture, or anything more than a steadfast, silently complicit denial of everything that is erupting around us, all the horrors done in our name, if our lives are to be based on that which is real, that which feels, that which weeps, that which rages; if life is to be based on truth and justice, a truth and a justice that thunders with a sound and a fury that signifies everything that is really real, then this life will be difficult, difficult, most difficult. Do you miss her?

(Robert nods, holding back tears.)

DOUGLAS: Well, we have to stay awake.

(Robert shakes his head like a child.)

DOUGLAS: We have to stay awake.

ROBERT: I don't want to stay awake.

DOUGLAS: Well, we have to stay awake.

ROBERT: I don't want to stay awake.

DOUGLAS: We have no choice.

ROBERT: We have no choice?

DOUGLAS: We have no choice.

ROBERT: We have no choice?

DOUGLAS: We have no choice.

ROBERT: We have no choice?

DOUGLAS: We have no choice!

ROBERT: We have no choice.

DOUGLAS: We have no choice.

End

Bibliography

Bakan, Stasiulis, ed. *Not One of the Family: Foreign Domestic Workers in Canada*. Toronto: University of Toronto Press, 1997.

Bannerji, Himani. *Thinking Through: Essays on Feminism, Marxism and Anti-Racism*. Toronto: Women's Press, 1995.

Lee, Butch and Red Rover. *Night Vision: Illuminating War and Class on a Neocolonial Terrain*. New York: Vagabond Press, 1993.

Churchill, Ward. *Indians Are Us? Culture and Genocide in Native North America*. Toronto: Between The Lines, 1994.

Churchill, Ward. *Since Predator Came: Notes from the Struggle for American Indian Liberation*. Colorado: Aigis Publications, 1995.

Churchill, Ward. *Struggle for the Land: Indigenous Resistance to Genocide, Ecocide, and Expropriation in Contemporary North America*. Toronto: Between The Lines, 1992.

Cole, Gittens et al., Commissioners. *Report of the Commission of Systemic Racism in the Ontario Criminal Justice System*. Toronto: Queen's Printer, 1995.

Fine, Weis, Powel, and Wong, eds. *Off White: Readings on Race, Power and Society*. New York: Routledge, 1997.

Monet, Don and Skanu'u. *Colonialism on Trial*. Gabiola Island, B.C.: New Society Publishers, 1992.

Mukherjee, Arun. *Oppositional Aesthetics: Readings from a Hyphenate Space*. Toronto: TSAR Publications, 1994.

Sakai, J. *Settlers: The Mythology of the White Proletariat.*

Silvera, Makeda. *Silenced: Talking With Working Class Caribbean Women about their Lives and Struggles as Domestic Workers in Canada.* Toronto: Sister Vision, 1993, 1989.

Spivak, Gayatri Chakravorty. *The Spivak Reader.* New York: Routledge, 1996.

Weatherford, Jack. *Indian Givers: How the Indians of the Americas Transformed the World.* New York: Ballantine, 1988.

West, Cornel. *Keeping Faith: Philosophy and Race in America.* New York: Routledge, 1993.

West, Cornel. *Race Matters.* Toronto: Random House, 1993.

WHO SHOT JACQUES LACAN?

Characters

ROSALBA is sexy, aloof, bitchy, impatient and mysterious. She wears a dress.

JACQUES is, at the beginning and end of the show, cocky and confident. All moments in between he is spineless, self-loathing, whimpering and frightened. Whenever he notices anyone other than Rosalba he seems to be confused as if he can't quite understand what they are doing there. He dresses nicely with a tie and suit jacket.

MARK J is introduced as Sigmund Freud and is to remain somewhat of an enigma except to speak the enigmatic line 'This thing speaks' – which is a reference to Freud's assertion that the unconscious is structured 'like a language'. He accompanies the entire performance with his drumming and, with a foot pedal, controls the halogen light.

THE BOYS are not literally boys; they are a small gang of well-dressed, Lacan-quoting, gun-toting thugs, each very different from the others:

JASON is an ominous fellow. He, though our audience will never know, is the archetypal figure of Death.

ANDREW is an intelligent fellow, supplying some of the more complicated quotes, controlling the light, and remaining fairly emotionless. He could be called the Scientist.

OWEN is an angry fellow. He instigates a couple of fights and, if the proper spots can be found, will start a few more and shoot his gun at the audience. In addition, he and MARK L (sometimes referred to as O & ML) provide the play with a small dance number and a bit of singing. He could be called Severity.

MARK L is kind of a simple thug. Somewhat of a keener, bright-tailed and bushy-eyed. He is excited to join with Owen to provide the play with dancing and singing. He could be called Mercy.

Set

The set features, at stage right, a microphone; upcentre is a carpet on which rests a chair and at stage left is a snare or some other kind of drum. A high-powered halogen lamp is also featured and is often in the hands of Andrew or at the feet of Rosalba.

Production History

Who Shot Jacques Lacan? was produced twice in 1994 by Mammalian Diving Reflex, featuring Park Bench, Andrew Kines, Mark Lonergan, Rosalba Martini, Owen Thompson, Jason Thompson and Mark Johnson, with direction by Darren O'Donnell and musical direction by Mark Johnson.

Prologue

(The Boys enter from the audience and set up the stage. Jason sets up the microphone and speaks during the setup.)

JASON: Ladies and ladies and gentlemen, please prepare, in the course of the next few minutes, yourself for …
A NO LOCO BAMBINO PRESENTATION OF THE PREMIERE PRODUCTION OF MAMMALIAN DIVING REFLEX'S PRESENTATION OF *WHO. SHOT. JACQUES. LACAN.*

Starring:

> Mr Mark Johnson as … the Four of Cups.
> Mr Andrew Kines as … the Six of Swords.
> Mr Mark Lonergan as … the Eight of Cups.
> Ms Rosalba Martini as … the Ace of Wands.
> Myself, Mr Jason Thompson, as … the Ten of Swords.
> My younger brother, Mr Owen Thompson, as … the Four of Disks.
> And introducing Mr Park Bench as … Jacques Lacan.

Mammalian Management by Ms Concetta Principe.
Musical Direction by Mr Mark Johnson.
And Written and Directed by Mr Darren O'Donnell.
With additional text by M Jacques Lacan.

Now, Ladies and ladies and gentlemen, in the way of pertinent support information I offer you the following:

M Jacques Lacan, born in 1901 and untimely cut down by an unknown assassin's bullet in 1981, was a French Freudian psychoanalyst, arguably one of the most radical yet influential thinkers of the 20th century. He was part of an extraordinary constellation of minds to emerge into prominence in France in the 1950s, a group that includes Lévi-Strauss, Althusser, Barthes and Foucault. Speaking in reference to M Lacan, the American linguist and media pundit Mr Noam Chomsky has said: 'My frank opinion is that Lacan was a conscious charlatan, and was simply playing games with the Paris intellectual community to see how much absurdity he could produce and still be taken seriously'. And, Ladies and ladies and gentlemen, Mr. Noam Chomsky is, between you and me, no deadbeat.

Now, Ladies and ladies and gentlemen, to avoid an insurgence of confusion I will provide you with one Interpretive Key. The Key is as follows: M Lacan says Herr Freud says, 'The unconscious is structured like a language' – i.e., the unconscious SPEAKS. So, that's the key, now it's up to you, our starving audience, to find the lock. Good luck. Ladies and ladies and gentlemen, may I now offer you ... *Who Shot Jacques Lacan? (pulls out his gun and shouts)* NOBODY MOVES NOBODY GETS HURT!

OWEN, MARK L and ANDREW: *(who have situated themselves in the audience since setting up the stage, whip out their guns and begin shouting)* Stay down, don't move, nobody move, nobody moves nobody gets hurt, stay down, careful, careful, no sudden gestures, nobody moves nobody gets hurt, easy does it, watch yourselves, nobody moves nobody gets hurt, nobody moves nobody gets hurt, nobody moves nobody gets hurt, nobody moves nobody gets hurt, nobody moves nobody gets hurt.

JACQUES: *(Enters from offstage and walks up to the microphone. He speaks into microphone)* Ladies and ladies and gentlemen, my name is Jacques Lacan, and, saaaay fellas, those fucking guns aren't LOADED ... are they?

(The Boys point their guns at the stage, adding a filmic sound effect.)

JACQUES: *(inhales with a mock shock, smiles and speaks)* I repeat – Ladies and ladies and gentlemen, my name is Jacques Lacan, and, saaaay fellas –

(The Boys shoot their indeed loaded guns at Jacques as many times as they can manage. It's a mob-style massacre. But Jacques manages to crawl his way out down the aisle of the audience and, depending on the theatre, out the door of the auditorium. One by one, the Boys, as each fires the last of his bullets, freeze. An ungainly silence ensues. Mark J enters quickly and heads straight to his drum[s]. Snap to black.)

Scene 1

(Mark J starts up on the skins.)

BOYS: *(pushing their way through the audience)*
     'scuse us, 'scuse us, 'scuse us
          'scuse me
     'scuse us, 'scuse us, 'scuse us
          'scuse me
     'scuse us, 'scuse us, 'scuse us
          'scuse me

(The Boys get to the stage and stand in a line. They pause, then quickly rifle through the following quote.)

One always knows enough in order to occupy the minutes during which one exposes oneself in the position of the one who knows enough in order to occupy the minutes during which one exposes oneself in the position of the one who knows. And we want to know: what do you know? What do you know? What do you know? We want to know: what do they know? What do they know? What do they know? We want to know: what do they know? What do they know? What do they know?

JASON: *(steps forward and speaks into the mike)* Thank you very much. And now, Ladies and ladies and gentlemen, I'd like to introduce to you, our starving audience, on the skins: Dr *(as an aside to the audience)* – you're not going to believe this – Dr Sigmund Freud.

(Mark does some riffing on the skins.)

BOYS: *(grinning like morons)* That's Sigmund Freud, Ladies and ladies and gentlemen.

JASON: It sure is, boys.

JACQUES: *(from offstage)* And I! *(Mark starts to build some sort of tension on the skins.)*

JASON: Oh, no, here he comes.

JACQUES: AND I!!

JASON: Nothin's gonna stop this cat.

JACQUES: AND I!!

BOYS: AND HE!

JACQUES: *(enters) AND I!*

BOYS: *AND HE!*

JACQUES: *AND I!*

BOYS: *AND HE!*

(Jacques enters and goes straight to the mike, pushing Jason out of the way. Jason tries to lunge at Jacques but the Boys hold him back. Mark J stops the drumming.)

JACQUES: And I ... am ... Jacques ... Lacan.

BOYS: And weeee don't ... like him.

(Jacques hits what could be described as an Elvis-like pose.)

(Blackout)

Scene 2

(Mark J resumes on the skins.)

(Andrew suddenly illuminates Jacques. Owen and Mark L stand by the microphone. Jason stands a little out of it and smokes a butt.)

JACQUES: A question suddenly arises.
　　　A question *(O & ML chime in)* suddenly arises.

JACQUES WITH O & ML: A question suddenly arises.
　　　A question suddenly arises.

MARK L: What's the question, Jacques?

OWEN: Yeah, tell us, Jacques.

JACQUES: YOU WANNA KNOW?

MARK L: WANNA KNOW?

JACQUES: YOU WANNA KNOW?

OWEN: WANNA KNOW?

JACQUES: YOU WANNA KNOW?

O & ML: *(they pause, look to each other, then speak)* WE GOTTA KNOW!

(Mark J stops.)

JACQUES: *(full of bravado)* In the case ... of the knowledge ... yielded solely to the subject's MISTAKE ... what kind of subject could ever be in a position to know it ... in advance?

(Owen and Mark L are shocked. What a question!)

JASON: Well, ummmm, *(Owen and Mark L are even more shocked by Jason's interruption and Andrew whips the light around and illuminates Jason)* that's easy ...

(Owen and Mark L are completely flabbergasted by Jason's outrageous assertion and Andrew, in direct response, simply turns off the light. Mark L resumes on skins and in the darkness Andrew drops the light off at Rosalba's feet.)

Scene 3

(Jacques is positioned stage left smoking a butt, preparing for the next scene; Mark L stands at the mike stand; Owen, Andrew and Jason stand behind Mark L.)

MARK L: Ladies and ladies and gentlemen ... *(indicating Rosalba)* Woman. *(He becomes unsure of himself, turns to the other Boys.)* Women? Woman? Women.

BOYS: *(trying to help)* Women, woman, women, woman *(etc.)*

MARK L: *(continuing to flounder)* Woman, women, women, woman ...

JACQUES: WOMEN!! *(pronounced like 'Wimmin')*

MARK L: *(indicating Rosalba)* Women. *(The light at her feet is activated.)*

JACQUES: *(to Rosalba, ignoring the Boys)* Um ... well ... if there was, you know, something, you know, something I could do to change things.

ROSALBA: *(sceptically)* And this escapes your mind?

JACQUES: *(grinning at the audience)* I wasn't even aware I had a mind.

ROSALBA: *(Owen slaps or punches Jacques viciously)* Don't mess around.

JACQUES: *(pouting, holding his face)* Mess around?

ROSALBA: You heard me.

JACQUES: No, you hurt me. *(Owen slaps him again.)*

JACQUES: I'm getting tired of this.

ROSALBA: I don't know what to say to you.

JACQUES: *(screaming)* SO DO YOU WANT ME TO KILL HIM?!! OKAY. I'LL KILL HIM!

JASON: *(into the microphone)* Um, can I get anybody a drink?

(Rosalba and Jacques obviously stiffen with a violent intake of air.)

JASON: *(with suspicion to the audience)* Something I said?

(Blackout)

Scene 4

(In the black the Boys all run upstage and get into somewhat of a chorus line. Rosalba turns on the light, Jacques falls to his knees and moves slowly towards Rosalba.)

BOYS: Unconscious desire proceeds by interpretation
Interpretation proceeds by
Unconscious desire proceeds by interpretation
Interpretation proceeds by unconscious desire

MARK L: *(Takes three strides away from the group moving stage left and collapses as Jacques, who has reached Rosalba, turns to face the audience. He speaks into his hands as Jacques mouths the words.)*

SO WHAT ARE YOU SAYING TO ME?!! ARE YOU TRYING TO TELL ME THAT MEANING INFINITELY EXCEEDS THE SIGNS MANIPULATED BY THE INDI-VIDUAL?!!

(Pause as the Boys look to each other in a kind of 'Yeah, sure, I guess so, why not' kind of way.)

ROSALBA: Yes.

MARK L: *(crying as Jacques lip-syncs)* BUT THAT MEANS I AM NOT WHAT I MEAN!!!!

(Mark J starts on skins. Andrew walks calmly to the mike.)

MARK L: Mean!!!! Mean!!!! Mean!!!!

ANDREW: Jacques! What we always must know is how to ignore what we know.

MARK J: *(punctuates the end of Andrew's sentence with a riff, and in the silence that ensues he speaks)* This. Thing. Speaks.

Scene 5

(Rosalba sits in chair and Jacques stands. Owen and Jason remain behind Rosalba, Mark L remains near Mark J and Andrew remains at the microphone. Rosalba and Jacques stare at each other. Tension fills the air. They both look hurt and angry. This drags on for a number of moments. Jacques has something wrong with his stomach. Rosalba finally breaks the silence.)

ROSALBA: Should I hold your head?

JACQUES: If you wouldn't mind. *(settles himself on Rosalba's lap)*

ROSALBA: I had a vision today.

JACQUES: *(no sarcastic intent)* Are you sure you weren't just seeing things?

ROSALBA: *(ignoring him)* An angel in the form of a scientist came to me and told me the following:

(Rosalba looks off into the distance as if remembering while Jacques alternates panic-stricken looks between Andrew, Rosalba and the audience.)

ANDREW: *(speaking into the microphone)* The written word was discovered by two young lovers.

ROSALBA: He told me that the written word was discovered by two young lovers.

ANDREW: *(into microphone)* After spending the weekend making love, they lay bathing in the sun. The strands of protein floating behind their closed eyelids, those strands of protein illuminated by the blazing sun provided a scriptic interpretation of the event.

ROSALBA: Love, sun and strands of protein invented the written word.

ANDREW: *(into microphone)* All subsequent efforts to use the written word to describe anything other than Love, Sun and Protein have, between you and me, failed.

Scene 6

JACQUES: You kill him, I can't.

ROSALBA: All right, I will.

JACQUES: No, I'll kill him!

ROSALBA: So kill him.

JACQUES: What if he kills me?

ROSALBA: Take him by surprise.

JACQUES: I'm not very good at surprises. *(to audience)* I have an honest face. It's a dead giveaway.

ROSALBA: Jacques, do you want me to kill him?

JACQUES: *(as Rosalba is quietly lifted straight upstage in her chair by Owen and Jason)* Okay, look, I, uh … it's like this: I'm a boy. A mere boy. I'm scared. He's a man. He looks mean. His fists are so big. My head is so small. He could crack my head in half. *(he collapses)* Oh please, I need to hide in you, pleeeeeease fill my mouth to stop my babbling with your piss!!!! *(he's a pathetic mess on the floor)*

Scene 7

(Andrew grabs the light, which has been at Rosalba's feet since Scene 3, and shines it onto Mark J as Owen moves downstage to join Mark L. Jason and Rosalba kiss quietly in the background.)

MARK J: *(while he provides his own accompaniment)* This thing speaks. This thing speaks. This thing speaks. This thing speaks I think I think I think I think this thing speaks. This thing speaks. This thing speaks. This thing speaks. I think I think I think I think this thing speaks.

(After a few rounds of the above Andrew shines the light on the collapsed Jacques, who stylistically discovers his hands drenched in [mime] blood then covers his eyes. Andrew turns out the light. This is repeated about three times with Andrew illuminating Jacques from different angles and Owen and Mark L starting the Thang Dance. Andrew then shines the light at Mark L and Owen who sing and do the Thang Dance.)

O & ML: Don't talk to us about hidden truth
    Don't talk to us about what's out there
    In the present we sing
    In the past we sang
    I've had about enough of this crazy thang!

    Don't talk to us about the essential self
    Don't talk to us about things that go bump
    If it was you called
    Then it was you who rang
    And I've had about enough of this crazy thang!

    Don't talk to us about Wilhelm Reich
    Don't talk to us about C.G. Jung
    One of them's Yin
    One of them's Yang
    I've had about enough of this crazy thang!

Scene 8

(Rosalba and Jacques are separated by a gulf – she at the back, he at the front. Andrew lights the scene from the centre. Owen and Mark L remain near Mark J and Jason remains standing behind Rosalba.)

JACQUES: *(talking to Rosalba but looking out into the audience – he is panicked from having just killed Him)* Yeah, uh-huh, okay. Okay. DONE!

ROSALBA: Done?

JACQUES: Done. Done, I've done it. *(frantically pats his body in search of the gun)* I can't find the gun!

ROSALBA: What?

JACQUES: THE GUN! I CAN'T FIND THE GUN!

ROSALBA: Where did you have it last?

JACQUES: When I shot him.

ROSALBA: *(losing her cool)* WHERE DID YOU PUT IT?!

JACQUES: Uh, I, uh …

ROSALBA: Yes?

JACQUES: I uh, I think I, uh …

ROSALBA: You think you what?

JACQUES: I put it, uh, *(with amazement)* I put it in his pants.

ROSALBA: *(incredulous)* You murdered a man then put the weapon in his pocket?!

JACQUES: *(amazed)* I put it in his pocket?

ROSALBA: What's the matter with you?

JACQUES: I don't remember putting it in his pocket. Who told you that?

(During the following dialogue Owen and Mark L cross between Rosalba and Jacques, meet with Jason directly between them. Andrew illuminates the meeting of the three men, for a moment forgetting about Rosalba and Jacques.)

ROSALBA: You did!

JACQUES: I did?

ROSALBA: You idiot!

JACQUES: When did I tell you that?

ROSALBA: JACQUES!

JACQUES: In his pants.

ROSALBA: What?

JACQUES: I said in his pants.

ROSALBA: His pants?

JACQUES: His pants.

ROSALBA: You ... what?

JACQUES: Put the gun in his pants.

ROSALBA: Not his pocket?

JACQUES: No, his pants.

ROSALBA: You undid his fly?

(The brief meeting between the Boys should be over. Andrew resumes illuminating the dialogue and Owen and Mark L head to the mike area while Jason heads stage left behind Mark J.)

JACQUES: I undid his fly –

ROSALBA: And you put the gun ...

JACQUES: – in his pants.

ROSALBA: Was he not wearing underwear?

JACQUES: Oh yeah, I put the gun inside his underwear ... right next to his, to his, to his ...

(pause)

ROSALBA: Penis?

BOYS: *(coughing the word into their hands)* PENIS!

JACQUES: Yeah, that.

(pause)

ROSALBA: Why?

JACQUES: Well … it reminded me of … something.

Scene 9

OWEN: You see, Jacques, there's one thing you've forgotten: the BODY moves faster than we THINK. Pun intended.

MARK L: *(to audience)* Who got the pun? Did anybody get it? Anybody, anybody? Get the pun? Anybody? Do you like theatre that makes you think?

(Owen solidly punches Mark L in the stomach. Mark retaliates and they begin a fairly vicious fight. Andrew abandons the light and goes to the microphone. Jacques picks up the light and illuminates the fight. Mark J does a drum solo which takes him into the audience. He uses the chairs, the floor, the audience's heads, all to create his percussive barrage. Jason walks into the audience and chants.)

JASON: I'm what happens in everybody else's head
And you're what happens in my head
I'm what happens in everybody else's head
And you're what happens in my head

ANDREW: *(speaks into the microphone during the fight, Jason's chant and Mark's solo)* The Freudian unconscious has nothing to do with the so-called forms of the unconscious that preceeded it and which still surround it today, forms of the unconscious which will tell nobody anything that they did not already know, and which simply designate the non-conscious, the more or less conscious, etc. Freud's unconscious is not at all the romantic unconscious of imaginative creation. It is not the locus of the divinities of the night. To all these forms of the unconscious, ever more or less linked to some will regarded as primordial, to something preconscious, what Freud opposes is the revelation *(he builds his passion)* that at the level of the unconscious there is something at all points homologous with what occurs at the level of the subject – THIS THING SPEAKS!

(By this time the fight has moved to stage left, and Jason has moved to stage right.)

JASON: *(into the microphone)* And if this thing speaks, I'll bet my number-one heart on you that this crazy ol' barn door can sing up a mean stir-fry. Let's listen:

O & ML: The shadow talks in languages
The shadow talks in languages
The shadow talks in languages
The shadow talks in languages
And you know what they say about languages
And you know what they say about languages
And you know what they say about languages
And you know what they say about languages

Scene 10

(Rosalba stands for the first time in the show and brings the chair up to Jacques, who remains near centre. He stumbles then sits. Andrew takes the light and illuminates Jacques and Rosalba. Jason remains at the microphone and Mark L and Owen remain stage left.)

JACQUES: They'll never know you were involved.

ROSALBA: I wasn't involved.

JACQUES: *(reminding himself)* Right, you weren't involved. Will they chop my head off?

ROSALBA: Idiot, they don't do that any more.

JACQUES: How then?

ROSALBA: By a firing squad.

JACQUES: They'll shoot me?

ROSALBA: All guns will have blanks but one.

JACQUES: So, nobody will know who shot me?

ROSALBA: Nobody.

O & ML: Who shot Jacques Lacan?
Who shot Jacques Lacan?
Who shot Jacques Lacan?
Who shot Jacques Lacan?

JASON: *(while Owen and Mark L chant)* To make a long story short. Standing in front of the firing squad he recognized HIM, the man he had supposedly killed. *(Jason takes out his gun and points it at the audience)*

JACQUES: *(staring out into the audience in amazement)* Hey! That's him! That's him! He's alive! I shot him! He's alive! He's alive! You're alive! You're alive! I've been framed, I've been framed, I've been framed, framed, framed, framed, framed, framed, framed ... *(continues to whisper throughout the final scene while Andrew pulls him gradually upstage on the chair leaving the light at Rosalba's feet)*

Scene 11

ROSALBA: *(to the audience)* My other lovers. *(with impatience)* Come on! Your reticence is fed by the moon ... and I howl at you. Listen to me, children: for three years things in life had reached a standstill. This I tell you for your own good. And this I tell you for it may be happening to you. And this I tell you from the only. Hole. Left. In. My. Trance. Zen. Den. Tall.

ROSALBA & BOYS: *(the Boys cough into their hands)* Heart.

ROSALBA: For three years things had reached an impasse, and gradually over the course of those three. Long.

BOYS: *(coughing)* Years.

ROSALBA: Over the course of these long years I noticed a man, why, he was an old FAMILY FRIEND. *(Andrew plays the part of the old family friend for a moment and walks down stage, picking up the light and illuminating Rosalba)* He would be there. At, say, a café, or say, a BOOK. LAUNCH. *(the Boys cough into their hands making the sound LAUNCH)* Or, say, sitting across from me at the dentist's office. And we would merely ... nod at each other. And so it happened on a hot summer night. Sitting at a café, or, say, sitting in the dentist's chair, or, say, standing at a BOOK. LAUNCH. *(the Boys cough into their hands making the sound LAUNCH)* it happened that this old family friend didn't nod at me. He walked right up to me. And he said to me ...

O & ML: *(singing)* Hot meals, salads and sandwiches.

(Andrew mouths the words as Jason speaks into the microphone.)

146

JASON: Um, I've been, um, authorized, I guess that would be the right word, um … to … uh. Oh, I'm sorry, how've you been doing?

ROSALBA: Fine.

JASON: No … uh … complaints?

ROSALBA: Why should I complain?

JASON: I dunno … it's what everybody else does.

ROSALBA: And they do it well.

JASON: Well, it's easy.

ROSALBA: Yes.

(a pause of the awkward kind)

O & ML: *(singing)* Hot meals, salads and sandwiches.

JASON: *(clears his throat)* Well … uh … like I was saying … I've been authorized to talk to you. To, uh, tell you that, well, things have come to a sort of standstill … for you. And I just wanted to let you … in … on why this is.

ROSALBA: At this point my old family friend stopped and, before my very eyes, like a greasy magician! He materialized, out of thin! air! a lit … cigarette.

(Mark J on skins.)

BOYS: *(singing)* Hot meals, salads and sandwiches. *(they repeat this until Jason returns to the stage)*

JASON: *(steps off the stage and quietly speaks to the audience. Andrew shines the light into the audience)* Can I get a smoke from somebody? And a light? Thanks. *(Back on stage speaking into the mike. As he smokes Andrew mimes smoking)* Look it, this is going to sound, kind of, I don't know, crazy, if I may be so bold as to use such a … loaded word but … you're dead, or 'already' dead, you have been … for these past three years.

(pause)

O & ML: *(singing)* Hot meals, salads and sandwiches.

ROSALBA: I noticed things had gone a bit stale.

JASON: Anyway, there you go, I've got to get back. I've got to get up in a few hours.

(He turns away from the mike.)

ROSALBA: Can I have the smoke?

JASON: Oh yeah, thanks. *(hands it to Andrew who hands it to Rosalba then speaks to the audience via the mike)* I always forget … and wake up with the bed on fire. Ciao.

(Jason waves, then freezes. Rosalba freezes in the middle of taking a drag; the ash grows longer throughout the final song.)

O & ML: *(singing at twice the speed of previous)*
        Hot meals, salads and sandwiches.
        Hot meals, salads and sandwiches *(etc.)*

(Jacques gets up and quickly walks to the mike, very much like he did at the beginning of the show. He shoves Jason away from the microphone; they get into a small scuffle and Jacques punches Jason deftly in the stomach. Jason collapses, then freezes. Andrew illuminates Jacques and perhaps O & ML as they sing.)

JACQUES: *(singing into the mike)* I am but a lonely dog.

O & ML: Ha da da da da
    Ha da da da da
    Ha   Ha Ha

JACQUES: I am but a weary frog.

O & ML: Ha da da da da
    Ha da da da da
    Ha   Ha Ha

JACQUES: I know things I'm not supposed to talk about
    I've heard rumours that I cannot afford to spread
    I know one or two things about you
    I have the sneaking suspicion that
    You and I are always already dead.

O & ML: Hot meals, salads and sandwiches.
    Hot meals, salads and sandwiches.

JACQUES: I am but an able mouse.

O & ML: Ha da da da da
    Ha da da da da
    Ha   Ha Ha

JACQUES: A crypt, a maze, a fully furnished house.

o & ml: Ha da da da da
  Ha da da da da
  Ha   Ha Ha

jacques: A likeness that you have no choice but to recreate
  A confusion with words to label what's already been named
  And insisting that monsters do not exist
  Reveals an opinion far more than itself
  That you and I are always already framed.

o & ml: Hot meals, salads and sandwiches.
  Hot meals, salads and sandwiches.

jacques: I am but an empty crate.

o & ml: Ha da da da da
  Ha da da da da
  Ha   Ha Ha

jacques: A twist of the wrist, a flick of fate.

o & ml: Ha da da da da
  Ha da da da da
  Ha   Ha Ha

jacques: A servant of God has all the power to retaliate
  And it took just a look to render and blend your face
  And if it turns out that the voice you call mine
  Situates itself at a particular point
  It's my proposal that time's been replaced by space
  Yes, my proposal that time's been replaced by space
  My humble proposal that time's been replaced by space.

(Jason unfreezes, stands, points his gun at Jacques. Jacques hits a pose. Owen and Mark L smile at the audience. The lights go out except for one on Rosalba. She unfreezes, extends her hand, making sure not to dislodge the ash on the cigarette. She lifts her index finger and pauses, poised, ready to bring it down and knock the ash.)

ROSALBA: The ego is itself structured like a symptom … inside the subject it is the human symptom par excellence. The ego … is human beings' mental illness.

(She brings her index finger down onto the smoke. The ash falls but before it hits the ground … blackout.)

End

(To the tune of Aerosmith's 'Back in the Saddle' the cast stands in a serious line for their bows. They take one, nice and slow, then another and, while in full bow they assume a friendly smile which is revealed to the audience once they stand straight. They slowly wave a salute to the audience, turn to their right and begin a very slow walk upstage. When they have almost reached the upstage wall they whip around, the Boys pointing their guns at the audience. The Boys move quickly downstage and Mark J steps in front of Rosalba and Jacques, pulls out a cigar, lights it, takes a puff, and the three begin a slow walk downstage. The Boys form a phalanx that guides Rosalba, Mark J and Jacques out through the audience and out of the theatre. Rosalba and Jacques smile benevolently at the audience, Jacques winks at a woman here and there, and the entire entourage heads slowly out the door with Jason, the figure of Death, being the last to leave. The house lights begin their slow ascent.)

RADIO ROOSTER SAYS THAT'S BAD

Characters

DR RADIO ROOSTER is a modestly arrogant member of the scientific community whose research is unknown to many. He enjoys himself always … and a little too much. He wears a blue polyester suit.

THE MOUSE resides inside Dr Radio Rooster. He embodies the paranoia and neuroticism that Radio refuses to feel. Even so, the Mouse is brimming with cockiness.

Set

The set is comprised of six areas.

1. The Spectrum consists of seven light bulbs – red, orange, yellow, green, blue, indigo and violet – dangling from the grid at chest level.
2. The Carpet area consists of a 4' x 8' rug, illuminated by two wicker lamps suspended from the ceiling by medium-width elastics which allow the lamps to bounce and twirl.
3. The Light Forest consists of four lamps arranged in a square that is approximately six feet per side.
4. The Desk features a desk upon which sits a glass of water and two small but very high-powered halogen lamps.
5. The Mouse Light is a bulb situated in the audience. It is delineated by a spotlight.
6. Centre Stage features a microphone lowered to waist level.

Production History

Radio Rooster Says That's Bad was produced twice at Buddies in Bad Times Theatre in 1994 by Mammalian Diving Reflex and featured Darren O'Donnell as Radio Rooster, with direction by Andrew Kines.

Seminar 1

(Music plays loudly as the audience enters. Technicians, including the actor who will eventually play Dr Radio Rooster, are setting up the set from scratch. They use a flash cube from a camera to charge the enormous amount of glow tape that dots the set. As they finish the set-up they wander off. The audience continues to enter, mingle and gossip amongst themselves. Eventually Dr Radio Rooster, a world-renowned scientist, stylishly dressed in a suit too large and too cheap, enters the space, does a quick check of the lights that occupy the space, and discovers, to his chagrin, that one of the bulbs on the Spectrum does not work. He quickly exits, re-enters and replaces the bulb. He exits. The audience continues to chat. Dr Rooster re-enters with a chair that he places at the Desk. He takes a final look at the set then bends forward at Centre Stage to speak into the mike.)

Good evening. This piece of music was specifically chosen. It was specifically chosen to manipulate your consciousness. How? Allow me to tell you. Science says that sound vibrates. And science says you vibrate. When the sound vibrations strike your body they produce a complementary vibration in your body. Upon vibratory adjustment, your biochemical component adjusts as well. This music has changed the chemical structure of your body, the chemical structure of your mind, the chemical structure of your consciousness. My name is Dr Radio Rooster, and I say, 'That's bad! That's bad! That's bad! That's bad!'

(The theatre is plunged into darkness. The music changes from the preshow to a loop of well-recognized Beatles music and Dr Radio Rooster quickly reappears in the Mouse Light.)

Ladies and Gentlemen, I've got something to tell you. And ladies and gentlemen, it's something you're gonna wanna hear. We will be beginning tonight's lecture in Toronto but, ladies and gentlemen, believe it or not, we're gonna be ending it in Vancouver or, depending on which way the wind blows, San Francisco. How? Allow me to tell you: through the modern miracle of 'elastomeric propulsion'. Before this evening's lecture a team of pulsating minds installed a widely acknowledged propulsion device beneath this very theatre. And, ladies and gentlemen, tonight we will be launching the theatre and together travelling through the arc of the parabola to safely land in Vancouver or, depending on which way the wind blows, Alaska. But first, to ensure audience safety, we must insist upon safety restraints. Audience! Prepare to be restrained! Commence restrainment!

(The good doctor takes a length of black party streamer and walks the length of the audience ensuring that they are tucked in safely for the duration of the show.)

Audience! Prepare for inflingment! And fling!

(The doctor runs completely upstage and hurls himself at the back wall. Before contact, however, the theatre is again plunged into darkness. The Beatles loop resumes and is just as suddenly cut off as Dr Rooster reappears at the Spectrum, turning each light on.)

Good evening, ladies and gentlemen. The lighting for this lecture was specifically chosen. It was specifically chosen to manipulate your consciousness. How? Allow me to tell you. Science says that light vibrates. Each colour vibrates at a different rate. And science says you vibrate. When colour rays strike your body they produce a complementary vibration in your body. Upon vibratory adjustment, your biochemical component adjusts as well. Light changes the chemical structure of your body, the chemical structure of your mind, the chemical structure of your consciousness. My name is Dr Radio Rooster, and I say, 'That's bad! That's bad! That's bad! That's bad!'

(Dr Rooster has turned the Spectrum off. The Beatles loop has resumed for the moment then is cut as the doctor is revealed in profile on the Carpet. He quotes from Michael Murphy's The Future of the Body.*)*

No general theory of human development can in good faith overlook the enormous witness to mystical cognition and other forms of metanormal abilities revealed by modern religious studies, physical research, anthropological studies of shamanism and other kinds of systematic inquiry into extraordinary experience. The evolving universe and the supernatural, however named, stand before us now as two inescapable facts.

(Blackout. And in the black we hear Radio's voice:)

Be Care Ful Be Cause There Is A
Baby on board, there's a baby, there's a baby.
There's a baby on board, there's a baby, there's a baby.
There's a baby on board, there's a baby, there's a baby.
There's a baby on board.
Did You Eat A.

(Dr Rooster snaps on the red light on the Light Spectrum.)

Now, science says: Red light has a vibratory rate of 6200–6700 Angstrom Units. This is now causing a reaction in your adrenal glands. Sensitive audience members should already be feeling this. Your adrenal glands affect your survival instinct and your self-commitment. An overabundance of red light can yield 'clairsmellen': the ability to detect meaning from smells. Not so unusual. Dogs do it all the time.

(Radio snaps off the light.)

And we're nothing if not dogs.

(He snaps the light back on and plays all the lights like a light xylophone.)

I'm a dog
I'm a good dog
I'm a dog
I'm a good dog
I'm a dog
I'm a good dog
Woof woof woof woof woof woof woof

Everytime I look at a woman, NO!
Everytime I look at a woman, NO!
Everytime I look at a woman, NO!
Everytime I look at a woman.

I'm a dog
I'm a good dog
I'm a dog
I'm a good dog
I'm a dog
I'm a good dog
Woof woof woof woof woof woof woof

Fortunately missed my head
They've got someone over there
If this is going to be a war
Then best to catch a train

'Cause I'm a dog
I'm a good dog
I'm a dog
I'm a good dog
I'm a dog

I'm a good dog
Everybody get in line

Why're you acting so surprised?
Why act so innocent?
Don't pretend that you are shocked
Stop faking your indignance

'Cause you're a dog
But you're a good dog
You're a dog
But you're a good dog
You're a dog
You're a good dog
Everybody face the facts

Catastrophe looms overhead
And that's no matter of opinion
Some remark you're better off dead
But that's no way to avoid dog dominion

White boy! Your time is done
Yeah, they've got us figured out
The next millennium belongs to someone else
And this ship will be pan-continental

But if you happen to be feeling bitter
I happen to have some valid advice
Oh, I know, I know, you didn't make this world
Yeah, that's real nice, but here's the advice:

Just duck! Just duck! Just duck! Just duck!

'Cause we're dogs
But we're good dogs
We're dogs
But we're good dogs
We're dogs
We're good dogs

Come on, everybody
I want some support
I want to be joined by all the men
If you rant along with me I'll give us a biscuit
And if you're real good I'll take us on a walk

'Cause we're dogs
We're good dogs
We're dogs
We're good dogs
We're dogs
We're good dogs
Woof woof woof woof woof woof woof

Everybody! Everybody!

Woof woof woof woof woof woof woof

All the men! All the men!

Woof woof woof woof woof woof woof

All the women! All the women!

Woof woof woof woof woof woof woof

Everybody! Everybody!

Woof woof woof woof woof woof woof

For a hundred points
Name a type of crime film
featuring
cynical malevolent characters
in a sleazy setting
and an ominous atmosphere
that is
conveyed by
shadowy photography
and foreboding
background
music

'good dog'

*(Dr Rooster snaps off the Light Spectrum, the Beatles loop resumes
and is quickly cut off as he is discovered standing shocked in the
Mouse Light. He stands with his hands at his chest, clenched like
little mouse paws. He speaks like a cartoon mouse with a vaguely
American accent. It's still Radio Rooster but now he has become a
mouse, for just these few moments in time.)*

What's there to be so self-conscious about? Seem's everybody's got
   their own opinion. It's just that there're not too many mouse-
   traps with cheese in them. These days everybody seems to be
   using peanut butter. It's not like I got a problem with peanut
   butter but cheese has holes in it and peanut butter, well, peanut butter sticks to the roof of your mouth making it very difficult
   to bark like a dog, unless you call the 'click' of stickin' peanut
   butter barkin' like a dog *(clicks his tongue)* ... snap ... nope, that
   don't sound like any member of the canine club I've met. Sounds
   like I'm a mouse with peanut butter stuck to the roof of my

mouth which, coincidentally enough, I am. You see, I never had that problem with cheese. Cheese goes down easy whereas peanut butter, well, peanut butter is enough to want to make you give yourself over to the cats. Now, cats, they know just how to keep a young mouse dangling on the edge of the abyss. If you speak my language.

(The light snaps to black and remains black as Radio's voice is heard.)

The evolving universe and the supernatural, however named, stand before us now as two inescapable facts.

(Radio appears on the Carpet as he turns on the bouncing lamps, sending them bouncing luxuriously. Throughout the folowing speech, from E. J. Gold's book The Human Biological Machine as a Transformational Apparatus, *Radio performs a dance of gestures. He is well aware of the complexity of the text and expects no one to grasp the whole, but hopes that, when combined with the visual impact of the dance, some of the ideas may, perhaps, lodge in the audience's unconscious … He can, after all, only hope.)*

Mental pictures are just a filing system, a way of assigning some grasp-able meaning to simple electrical potential so that the mental apparatus can keep track of the machine's field distortions in which memory is stored. If the mental apparatus didn't assign meaning and significance to these electrical anomalies, it would have no way of recalling memory, because without significance all field distortions look alike. After all, they're just lumps of energy in an energy field … a slight variation of grey in an ocean of grey. Experience itself, especially experience within the space-time matrix, is a way of labelling something that is happening to us on an electrical-mathematical level. Perceptual experience and analysis of our experience is just one of many possible ways of sorting it out, labelling it and filing it. Our whole voyage from birth to death and beyond is a way of seeing what is happening. We file our electrical experience in memory by assigning to each electrical event a definite, rememberable subjective tactile hallucination.

(Radio snaps off the bouncing lamps.)

Be Care Ful Be Cause There Is A

(Dr Rooster snaps on the orange light on the Colour Spectrum.)

Now, science says: orange light has a vibratory rate of 5900–6200 Angstrom Units. This is now causing a reaction in either your ovaries or your testicles, stimulating either estrogen or testosterone. Sensitive audience members should be enjoying this already. The level of sex hormone in your body determines, among other things, your emotional style. Development of this system can yield 'clairsentience', the ability to feel what others are feeling.

(Dr Rooster snaps off the orange light and speaks in the dark.)

So Be Care Ful.

Be Care Ful Be Cause There Is A

(The Good Doctor, throughout the course of the following short section, is situated in the Light Forest. He accentuates his words by turning on and off the various lights.)

Baby on board, there's a baby, there's a baby
There's a baby on board, there's a baby, there's a baby
There's a baby on board, there's a baby, there's a baby
There's a baby on board

Did You Eat A
did you eat a rattlesnake
did you eat a truck did you eat a truck
did you eat a rattlesnake
did you eat a truck

Be Care Ful Be Cause There Is A
Baby on board, there's a baby, there's a baby
There's a baby on board, there's a baby, there's a baby
There's a baby on board, there's a baby, there's a baby
There's a baby on board

Did You Eat A
did you eat a rattlesnake
did you eat a rattlesnake
did you eat a rattlesnake
did you eat a rattlesnake
did you eat a rattlesnake
did you eat a rattlesnake
did you eat a rattlesnake
did you eat a truck did you eat a truck
did you eat a rattlesnake
did you eat a truck

What I mean, of course, by 'rattlesnake' is the quantum transfor-
mative form known as the Kundalini located here at the base of
the spine. What I mean, of course, by 'truck' is the sensation
of being hit by the Kundalini before you're ready – *(prepares to
sneeze)* Ah Ah Ah. Schizophrenia.

did you eat a rattlesnake
did you eat a truck did you eat a truck
did you eat a rattlesnake
did you eat a truck

(Dr Rooster snaps off the Light Forest and speaks the following line in total darkness.)

Be Care Ful Be Cause There Is A

(Dr Rooster casually sits at the Desk, turning the two halogen lights on. He wipes the sweat from his brow – it's been a rousing lecture thus far – and takes a sip of water. Once settled, he speaks.)

If one accepts the virulent nature of language
one must further accept that personality is a disease

because it's just me and you
and everybody and us
and what the hell what the hell

just me and you and everybody and us
and what the hell what the hell

as the children fast
faster and faster
and we continue to hurtle and hurtle

(At this point – and at all 'who's calling you's – he points the blindingly bright halogen lights at the audience, trying to focus on friends, familiar faces and the occasional critic.)

who's calling you
who's calling you

as you close down your mouth
and you shut down your eyes
and oh
and oh

and oh
and thunder
and lightning
rain from the skies

who's calling you
who's calling you

you can look to the East
you can look to the West
but best you hunker down, little ones,
and look deep
yeah deep

into the eyes of the ones you love best

'cause if it looks like rain
it must be water

and if it looks like snow
the same applies and applies and applies

so just who's calling you
who's calling you

lie down, little ones, way down.

(Dr Rooster lays his head on his Desk, snaps off the lights and speaks, albeit briefly, in the dark.)

did you eat a rattlesnake or did you eat a truck
did you eat a rattlesnake or did you eat a truck
did you eat a rattlesnake or did you eat A

(Dr Rooster is discovered like a startled mouse standing in the Mouse Light, his hands clenched like mouse paws. He speaks in his mouse dialect.)

What's there to be so self-conscious about? Seems everybody's got their own opinion. It's just that there are not too many mouse-traps with cheese in them. These days everybody seems to be using little chunks of greasy apple. It's not like I got a problem with little chunks of greasy apple, it's just that, well, cheese has holes in it and little chunks of greasy apple, well, with little chunks of greasy apple the peel's always getting stuck between your teeth, making it very difficult to smile for the camera. Unless, of course, you're prepared for a negative reaction. But when's the last time you saw a mouse with enough fortitude to take the time necessary to prepare for a negative reaction? Never! And this is one mouse who ain't about to break with tradition. You see, I never had that problem with cheese. Cheese goes down easy whereas little chunks of greasy apple, well, little chunks of greasy apple are enough to make you want to move out and make way for the cockroaches. Now, cockroaches, that particular species invented the negative reaction. If you speak my language.

(The light snaps out, the Beatles loop resumes and Radio is discovered in the Light Forest.)

Now, science says our fundamental building block is building block DNA. And science says DNA is composed of the ubiquitous carbon atom. And science says the carbon atom contains six protons, six neutrons and six electrons. Six protons, six neutrons and six electrons. Now, science is currently telling us that

The Devil's got plans for you and I
Raise your hands up high

The Devil's got plans for you and I
Raise your hands up high

It gets hard to move as soon as you should with a proper clock
It's to some degree whether or not a propensity docks
on a mother shoal 'cause that's my goal way way back in time

I seem to recall a distant voice I now confuse with mine
and the Devil jumps in whenever he can to kindly remind me
he's mine he's mine all mine the Devil is mine from way way back
    in time

yeah in time

in time

in time

yeah in time

The Devil's got plans for you and I
Raise your hands up high

The Devil's got plans for you and I
Raise your hands up high

The Devil's got plans for you and I
Raise your hands up high

The Devil's got plans for you and I
Raise your hands up high

Now, science says: yellow light has a vibratory rate of 5600–5900
    Angstrom Units. This is now causing a reaction in your pancreas,

stimulating insulin. Sensitive audience members should already be feeling this. Insulin metabolizes carbohydrates, giving you physical power and since everything is, conveniently, a metaphor for everything else, the colour yellow also gives you personal power. Warning! Development of this will yield the ability of 'telekinesis'.

(Radio shoots a telekinetic look offstage and a crash is heard.)

Oh ho ho ho. Yellow is also fundamental in the creation of mental maps which conceptually account for phenomena occurring Out there! Out there? In here out there in here out there in here out there in here out there in here out there in here out there in here.

(He snaps off the yellow light and then snaps on the halogen lamps on the Desk. He sits. He is not casual. He sings.)

Take a look at the fear in someone's eyes
Take a look at the fear in someone's eyes
Take a look at the fear I cannot disguise
That's it
all the fault of the secret service American agent man
That's it
all the fault of the secret service American agent man
That's it
all the fault of the secret service American agent man
That's it
all the fault of the secret service American bicentennial secretarial
    plan
That's it
all the fault of the overrated and underachieving wrist watch-
    twisting clan
That's it

all the fault of the Heritage Front and their not-so-secret plan
That's it
all the fault of the women and men who said they can't but can
That's it
all the fault of the mothers and daughters of the revolutionarial, curatorial, history of man scam
That's it
all the fault of the lights on the CN Tower and their effects on my brain pan
That's it
all the fault of the Christian cult and the veins on the back of my hand
That's it
all the fault of my bubbling double living in the jungles of Vietnam
That's it
all the fault of the Devil and God that divided and won my man

(Dr Rooster snaps off the halogen lights and in the darkness recites what is known as THE OBLIGATORY READER'S INVOCATION from E.J. Gold's American Book of the Dead. *As he recites he walks slowly throughout the space as close to, and preferably behind, the audience. He is very careful to make sure that the sound of his shoes on the floor resonates with a sombre tone.)*

to the divine silence of unreachable endlessness
to the divine silence of perfected knowledge
to the divine silence of the soundless voice
to the divine silence of the heart of the labyrinth
to the divine silence of the ancient mind
to the divine silence of the unborn guide
to the divine silence of the unseen guide, protector of all sentient life
to the divine silence of those of perfected knowledge

to the divine silence of human primate incarnation
to the divine silence of the labyrinth guides who have sacrificed
their liberation for those who have not yet awakened to the
truth
to the divine silence of the lord of death the eternal unborn resident of the labyrinth who has sacrificed her own redemption
for the redemption of all voyagers everywhere
to the divine silence of the primordial being
to the divine silence of the great sacrifice
we offer homage love and hope
but above all we give our gratitude.

Thanks … for nothing. for nothing for nothing for nothing for nothing for nothing

*(Lights up on audience … red. Radio stands among the audience.
After each question, he extends the microphone, but before an audience member can answer, there is a blackout.)*

Do you remember your dreams?

(Blackout)

(Lights up … orange)

While you dream are you aware you're dreaming?

(Blackout)

(Lights up … yellow)

Have you considered the possibility that we enter each other's
dreams?

(Blackout)

(Lights up ... blue)

If we accept the hypothesis that dreams can be cohabited how does this affect your approach to bedtime? Will you be sure to brush your teeth? Kiss me. Kiss me. Kiss me. Kiss me. Kiss me. Kiss me. Kiss me. Kiss me.

(Blackout)

(Radio appears on the Carpet. He quotes from E.J. Gold's The Human Biological Machine as a Transformational Apparatus *and does his dance of gestures,)*

The electrical field of the machine has no meaning in itself ... it's just a moving, swirling, ever-changing pool of dancing electrons, and things happen to the electrical field, forming electrical eddies, ridges and cataracts. As this happens, tactile hallucinations explain what is happening electrically. Every event is an electrical event completely devoid of any objective significance. We mustn't trust the hallucinations, the significance of which forms the subjective result we call personal experience, to tell us what really happened; we must trust the raw electrical memory itself, which we can follow if we have the training and disciplined skill to observe events in their pure electrical state.

(Dr Rooster snaps off the lamps and walks through the darkness, speaking.)

To the divine silence of the labyrinth guides who have sacrificed their liberation for those who have not yet awakened to the truth.

(Again he is discovered in the Mouse Light, in Mouse Posture, using the Mouse Voice.)

What's there to be so self-conscious about? Seems everybody's got their own opinion. It's just that there are not too many mouse-traps with cheese in them. These days everybody seems to be using slices of pumpkin pie. It's not like I got a problem with slices of pumpkin pie, it's just that, well, cheese has holes in it and slices of pumpkin pie, well, slices of pumpkin pie contain the mystical ingredient nutmeg, causing this particular rodent to suffer hallucinations. And not just any hallucinations. I start to think I'm a cat. But not just any cat. I think I'm a goddamn cat with a goddamn furball and, frankly, furballs hurt! I never had that problem with cheese. Cheese goes down easy whereas slices of pumpkin pie, well, slices of pumpkin pie, beyond the obvious menace of an hallucinatory furball, leave me craving a freshly killed mouse. And I swear I'll never eat my own species. If you speak my language.

(The theatre is again overtaken with darkness as Dr Rooster intones the following lines.)

To the divine silence of the Lord of Death. The eternal unborn resident of the labyrinth who has sacrificed her own redemption for the redemption of all voyagers everywhere. Everything. Everywhere. Everything. Everywhere. Everything.

(Radio snaps on the green bulb in the Spectrum.)

Green light has a vibratory rate of 5100–5600 Angstrom Units. This is now causing a reaction in your thymus gland, affecting your immune system. Sensitive audience members should be feeling healthier already. Development of this system allows you to sense what others are feeling and thinking. Not feel, but sense. The difference: benevolent detachment.

(Radio snaps off the green light and speaks in darkness.)

everything everything everything everything everything every-
thing everything everything everything

(Radio snaps on the halogen lights and sits at the Desk.)

While scrying in the spirit vision, I received the following information:

the DNA code is off its track
how're we gonna get the DNA code back

the DNA code is off its track
how're we gonna get the DNA code back

There's a war in heaven
There's a war in heaven
There's a war in heaven
There's a war in heaven

as above so below
as above so below
as above so below
so below
so below

the DNA code is off its track
how're we gonna get the DNA code back

I am not me I am them
I am not me I am them
I am the 'they' in 'That's what they say'
If you missed it the first time I'll say it again

the DNA code is off its track
how're we gonna get the DNA code back

Everybody's circling the same thing
Everybody's circling the same thing
Everybody's circling the same thing
Everybody's circling the same thing

And God is a lost continent
in the human mind

And God is a lost continent
in the human mind

And God is a lost continent
in the human mind

And God is a lost continent
in the human mind

And God is a lost continent
in the human mind

as above so below
so below
so below

the DNA code is off its track
how're we gonna get the DNA code back

You are not you
you are not them
you are them
you are the 'they' in 'That's what they say'
if you missed it the first time I'll say it again

And God is a lost continent
in the human mind

And God is a lost continent
in the human mind

And God is a lost continent
in the human mind

And God is a lost continent
in the human mind

We are not we
we are them
we are not we
we are them we are not we
we are them
we are the 'they' in 'That's what they say'

*(Dr Radio Rooster snaps off the halogen lights and in the darkness
stands at Centre Stage speaking the following text from Michael
Murphy's* The Future of the Body. *As he does this the lights slowly
rise, followed by the slow ascent of the Beatles loop.)*

No. General. Theory. Of human. Development. Can. In good faith.
Overlook. The enormous. Witness. To. Mystical. Cognition.
And other. Forms of Meta. Normal. Abilities. Revealed. By
modern. Religious. Studies. Psychical. Research. Anthro.
Pologi. Cal. Studies. Of. Sha. Man. Ism. And other kinds of
systematic inquiry. Into. Extra. Ordinary. Experi. Ence. The.
Evolving. Universe. And the. Super. Natural. Stand. Before us.
Now. As two. In. Escapable. Facts. The. Evolving. Universe.
And the. Super. And may I go so far as to say 'Duper'. Natural.
Stand. Before us. Now. As two. In. Escapable. Facts.

(Blackout. The Beatles loop is brought to a deafening pitch, then is just as suddenly extinguished. Silence. The lights rise slowly but Dr Radio Rooster is nowhere to be seen. Oh, there he is, lying on the floor speaking into the microphone.)

Gradually people, one by one, are becoming a consciousness quite detached from the functions of the body. Your body is beginning to take over and continues to operate within the set parameters of its already established routine with only small gradual changes over the course of many years. Every bodily function, every function of physical manifestation, is becoming automated and consciousness remains trapped, as if in a machine that takes you to you know not where. For example: you wake in the morning not knowing when your body will decide to get up, if it feels like a shower that morning, will you eat, once the food was in your mouth you cannot even be certain if you will eventually end up swallowing or would your fully automated body spit out the food. Your body communicates with other bodies the same as it had before but, again, you have no control, or choice, about what is said or with what emotion or intent it is being said. You are condemned to spend the rest of your physical life observing your body as it mechanically continues on its journey. Once in a while you can get some respite by curling up your terrified consciousness and resting it here, under the tongue, like a pearl, in the body that has become your prison.

As more and more people begin to discover themselves in this state we will find our bodies organizing ourselves in silent groups. Sometimes walking down the street, in a park, at the county fair. Sometimes we will arrive at an unfamiliar apartment to discover four other people sitting in silence. We will join them, sit in silence until, presumably we have had enough, then we will get up and leave. Sometimes two people set off to see a play, end up separating, sitting in rooms with strangers for four hours, then meet in a café to have an alarmingly in-depth discussion about the play that had never been seen. The only indication that things have gone awry is a slight glimmer of panic that begins to develop in your eyes. But no one ever makes mention of the problem, the newspapers never report it, the mail never stops, families continue to be fruitful and multiply.

(Blackout. Radio appears at the Light Spectrum, having snapped on the blue light.)

Now, science says: blue light has a vibratory rate of 4700–5100 Angstrom Units. This is now causing a reaction in your thyroid and parathyroid glands which, in turn, fine-tune your nervous system. Sensitive audience members should be feeling more and more calm. As your system calms be aware of increased 'clairaudience', the ability to hear sounds not within the time-space matrix.

(Radio snaps off the blue light and appears in the Mouse Light, acting like a mouse.)

I know what you're thinking. You're asking yourself how can this particular mouse continually gorge him- or herself – since in the mouse kingdom gender is a matter of preference and, frankly, I keep changing my mind, but nevertheless – how can this mouse consume such high-cholesterol items as little chunks of greasy apple, peanut butter and slices of pumpkin pie while all the while remaining so utterly lithe? The answer is simple: I got a tapeworm. And not just any tapeworm but an articulated tapeworm. And not just any articulated tapeworm but an articulated tapeworm who has recently assumed the name Righteous Indignation. Yessiree, you heard it direct from the mouse's mouth: I got an articulated tapeworm named Righteous Indignation and that's what keeps me lookin' so sexy skinny.

(Blackout. Radio appears on the Carpet, having activated the bouncing lamps.)

To observe events in their pure electrical state one must have a certain amount of training in a discipline. Most of the machine's activities the machine performs in secret from us. The machine drinks without our attention, eats without our attention, even makes love without our attention. To begin the process of accessing the shifts of energy on our energy field is to gain access to our attention. Now, ladies and gentlemen, what I am about to reveal is a highly effective means of accessing the power of attention. Those audience members with the disciplined skill to employ this technique will be highly rewarded by the results. But you must be warned: the exercise should only be performed by those of you who desire a total revolution which will place you irreversibly on the path to the palace of the pumpkin pie. Are you ready for the technique? Here! Is! Le technique! In your day-to-day activities simply regard the ambient honks of car horns that drift to you from off the streets as psychic confirmations of whatever you happen to be thinking at the time. Every honk of a horn is a comment from the void on whatever happens to be passing through your addled brain. Triple honks are particularly fortuitous.

Ah ah ah. Schizophrenia. Excuse me.

(Blackout. He extinguishes the lamps and moves to the Mouse Light, but speaks as Radio.)

And now, ladies and gentlemen,
we have a special, ladies and gentlemen, treat.

Tonight we will attempt to invoke the presence of a very dear friend of mine. So, please prepare a warm space in your large intestine for Righteous Indignation. As special enticement it becomes necessary to suspend a fraction of bacon from a string: thusly. Ladies and gentlemen, if all goes well, Righteous Indignation.

(Dr Rooster raises his hand high and holds a piece of cardboard bacon in front of his open mouth. He stands waiting for the appearance of the tapeworm. He very deliberately accentuates his breathing to create a sound that a large dragon might make while sleeping. Off in the distance we hear, first quietly, then louder and louder:)

BOYS: Da da da da
    Da da da da
    Da da
    Da da da

(Jason enters, goes up to Radio Rooster and frisks him, finding a pack of smokes. He lights one up. Radio is stuck in his position of holding the bacon.)

    I wanna girl
    Just like the girl
    That married dear old Dad

RR: Everything, everything, everything kills me
    Why can't I find anything that will not kill me?

(Rosalba enters and pumps a bullet into Radio Rooster.)

BOYS:Da da da da
    Da da da da
    Da da
    Da da da

(Jason takes a chair from the audience, asking that audience member to get out for a moment and sit in the aisle. He picks Radio up and sets him onto the chair.)

JASON: Can we have this seat? You can sit in the aisle, shit-for-brains! Take it away, Boys!

JACQUES: *(quickly enters and goes to mike)* Can I please have everybody relaxed. *(everybody disperses)* Smoke?! You can smoke.

OWEN: *(to audience)* Hey, he says we can smoke. *(lights one up himself)*

JACQUES: AND NUMBER ONE!

MARK L: Radio Rooster is a breath of flesh air for the beleaguered masses.

JACQUES: NUMBER TWO!

OWEN: Radio Rooster knows what to say and how to say it.

JACQUES: NUMBER THREE!

MARK J: Radio Rooster is fit to be friend. I'd fuck him!

JACQUES: And, ladies and gentlemen, NUMBER THREE! MOVES! TO!

ANDREW: He's talking about number three.

MARK L: We've mentioned three four times.

JACQUES: NUMBER FOUR!

JASON: Radio Rooster slipped a five-year-old child an exploding wristwatch.

JACQUES: The result?

JASON: The kid waxes philosophical and has been quoted as saying, 'While it may be true that two arms are better than one, an exploding watch, though it limits options, completely reiterates what we've all been feeling all along.'

JACQUES: And what's that?

JASON: BANG!

JACQUES: You said it. NUMBER FIVE!

ROSALBA: *(in Italian or Spanish)* Radio Galla Hatchacha!

JACQUES: AND SIX!

MARK J: WAKE UP WAKE UP WAKE UP!

(Radio Rooster wakes up with a start, sees his own death, and just as suddenly snaps out of it.)

RR: Welcome to my laboratory. *(claps his hands three times)* What we have here, see, is a simple apparatus, revolving around a number of simple, say, principles, principles, yes, principles. *(checks his suit pocket)* Who took my smokes?

ROSALBA: What Dr Rooster is trying to say is that though smoking increases the risk of heart disease he chooses to serve his tobacco addiction by continuing to smoke while at the same time hiring men to steal his cigarettes.

RR: It works, it really works! Oh, technician! Oh, stage manager! Can we have what we call in show biz … any guesses, any guesses, any guesses?

MARK L: A crossfade?

RR: No.

MARK J: Music cue?

RR: Uh uh.

JASON: A preset?

RR: Close.

OWEN: Does it have to do with lights or sound or both?

RR: Oh, that would be far too easy.

JACQUES: Dr Rooster?

RR: Yes, Dr Lacan?

JACQUES: Is the word you're looking for … blackout?

(Lights snap to black.)

BOYS: Da da da da
    Da da da da
    Da da
    Da da da

(They move the singing to a nauseatingly hipster kind of thing. Lights snap up on RR.)

RR: My name is Dr Radio Rooster and I say that's phat, that's real phat, real phat, real phat!

JACQUES: So, what's happening, Daddy-O?

RR: Oh, you know, not much, not much, not much.

JACQUES: Yeah?

RR: Howz about yourself?

ROSALBA: *(pops on indigo light and speaks in either Italian or Spanish)* Indigo light has a vibratory rate of between –

JACQUES: Oh, you know, can't complain.

ROSALBA: – 4500–4700 Angstrom Units.

RR: Who'd listen?

ROSALBA: This is now causing a reaction in your pineal gland, located here.

BOYS: *(quiet)* Don't talk to us about hidden truth.

RR: Who's talking about hidden truth?

BOYS: Don't talk to us about what's out there.

JACQUES AND RR: *(look to each other)* Out there?! Whoa, baby!

ROSALBA: Sensitive audience members should be noticing a significant rise in their intuitive intelligence.

BOYS: In the present we sing, in the past we sang, I've had about enough of this crazy thang.

(Blackout except for the indigo bulbs.)

ROSALBA: *(in English)* A rise in your intuitive intelligence can, watch out, result in clairvoyance.

BOYS: *(moving forward)*
Don't talk to us about the essential self
Don't talk to us about things
that
go
bump.
If it was you who called
then it was you who rang
and I've had about enough
of this crazy thang.

ROSALBA: *(in English)* According to the theories of Wasson, Allegro, Ruck and Hofmann, there is increasing evidence that all, not some, but all of the world's major religions were founded by cultures that had a symbiotic relationship with hallucinogenic plant life.

RR: Really? But the world's major religions are a mess.

ROSALBA: Mess. Yes.

RR: So?

ROSALBA: So.

BOYS: SO?! *(quickly)* Don't talk to us about Aldous H,
don't talk to us about Timothy L,
One of them's yin, one of them's yang,
I've had about enough of this crazy thang.

(Blackout. Lights up.)

RR: I laugh at myself to pass the time and to boost my endorphins.

ROSALBA: A rise in your intuitive intelligence can, watch out, result
in clairvoyance.

JACQUES: Does your laughter originate from a view of yourself that
you call your own or from an imaginary third person?

RR: Like who?

JACQUES: Like a multidisciplinary deity.

RR: Like a God?

JACQUES: But a God of many disciplines.

RR: Disciplines? Name three.

BOYS: We've mentioned three six times.

JACQUES: ONE!

BOYS: I wanna God just like the God that ... OH SWEETHEART!

JACQUES: AND A TWO!

BOYS: I wanna God just like the God that … OH HONEY-BUNCH!

JACQUES: AND A THREE!

BOYS: I wanna God just like the God that … OH PUMPKIN MOON PIE!

RR: Oh, I see what you mean, Dr Lacan, sure that's exactly where my self-effacing laughter originates.

BOYS: LET'S HEAR IT, DOCTOR R!

(RR starts to laugh like crazy, then they all laugh hysterically and stumble their way upstage.)

RR: Oh, you're too much.

ROSALBA: Dr Rooster! Oh, Radio Rooster. Tell us about hallucinations.

RR: Oh …

ALL: Ah Ah Ah.

RR: That's easy.

ALL: Choooooooooo!

(Blackout. Radio lights a candle which has materialized on the Desk.)

Ladies and gentlemen. To perceive is to respond electrically to stimuli. How much you perceive is contingent upon the quality of equipment you possess. No one person in this room sees the flame end at the same point. In fact those individuals with an overabundance of the powerful neurotransmitter serotonin, those individuals in our culture assigned the title schizophrenic, may actually be seeing the flame end here. Or here. Or here. And the flame does end there. It's just the rest of us who end somewhere around … oh, I don't know … here.

(Radio extinguishes the candle and snaps on the violet light in the Spectrum.)

Now, science says: violet light has a vibratory rate of 4000–4500 Angstrom Units. This is now causing a reaction in your pituitary gland located deep in the centre of your brain. Sensitive members of the audience will be able to feel the pituitary gently secreting serotonin. And as science says, serotonin is a powerful neurotransmitter. Serotonin allows your brain to communicate faster, thereby allowing you to hear faster, feel faster, taste faster, smell faster and see faster.

(Dr Rooster, leaving the violet light on, makes his way to Centre Stage.)

Two final points:

1. Ultraviolet light also increases the production of serotonin in your brain. And …
2. As we continue to reap the benefits of increased exposure to ultraviolet light we all may start to exist – ah ah ah choo – just a little too fast.

My name is Dr Radio Rooster and I say:

Look at the light don't look at the light!

(Before he can say anything he stops, reaches up and pulls down a bare white bulb that dangles from a long orange cord. This light is a surprise, never having been used or referred to. He turns on the light and begins the final illumination using the bulb as if it were a microphone.)

Jesus was a man and real men don't eat meat. The simple fact of the matter is matter can be beat. If it looks like rain it must be water, if it looks like snow the same applies, if it's nothing to do with you or me then step right up and lick my eye. The Devil needs a helping hand and Christ could use one too. If it looks like piss it must be water but just between you and me it looks like poo through and through. If the government had a better plan I'm sure they'd let us know, say, if we inhaled one final breath and all refused to blow. Just accuse yourself of anger, accuse yourself of sin, accuse yourself of sitting on the shelf after everyone else dove in. The Mother of it all hovers ready to SUCK US UP, the Father of it all shivers cursing HIS DUMB LUCK, but now we tuck the children in bed and let the adults die (as if there wasn't enough thunder rumbling in the empty sky). I look to you and you look to you and we let the others go, if we can make sense of all this mess I'm sure the plants will grow. But if it looks to you a troublesome picnic and looks to you a worrisome curse then it looks to me like murder-in-the-meantime and no one else can interpret worse. No one else can read the Bible, no one else can stomp it out, no one else can flirt with the Devil, and no one else gets hurt. No one else gets hurt. No one else gets hurt. No one else gets hurt. No one else gets hurt. I'LL MAKE YOU ONE LAST PROMISE AND I'LL MEAN IT. No one. Else gets … Ho! Ho! Ho! It's the legal representatives of Jesus Christ through the blizzard and the snow and he knows he knows he knows how to plough it home. Just twist the wrist that bites the hand that feeds the dog that barks into the eternal void. Come on! Come on! Come on! CLEAR! CLEAN!

(Dr Rooster now tosses the bulb into the air and, holding on to the cord, spins it furiously around his head. He eventually reels the bulb in and speaks.)

The temperature in Vancouver is currently hovering in and around the freezing point and the time is merely a matter of opinion ... thank you.

(He snaps off the light, making it clear that this is the end of the lecture proper. The audience does their job and applauds, Dr Rooster does his bows. He then asks for silence. He speaks.)

Throughout the course of my humble lecture I have used a variety of devices. To name a few: rhythm, rhyme and repetition, not to mention alliteration. So that's four devices: rhythm, rhyme, repetition and alliteration. Why rhythm, rhyme, repetition and alliteration? For a simple purpose: inoculation. Why inoculation? Because we're sick. What are we sick with? Our selves. A seeming fact deludes us while a simple fact eludes us.

Seeming fact A: I am not you I am me.

Simple fact B: I am not me I am thee.

Through rhythm, rhyme, repetition and alliteration it has been my intention to have you leave the theatre humming. If I have been graceful enough to wire any of my repetitive rhythmical rhymes into your mental circuitry, know this: you have been inoculated. Against what? Your self.

My name is Dr Radio Rooster and I say that's bad.

End

Bibliography

Alli, Antero. *Angel Tech*. Phoenix: New Falcon Press, 1985.

Buckland, Ray. *Practical Color Magick*. St Paul: Llewellyn Publications, 1983.

Felman, Shoshana. *Jacques Lacan and the Adventure of Insight*. Cambridge: Cambridge University Press, 1987.

Gold, E.J. *The Human Biological Machine as a Transformational Apparatus*. Nevada City: Gateways/IDHHB Inc., 1986.

Gold, E.J. *The American Book of the Dead*. Nevada City: Gateways/IDHHB Inc., 1987.

Grof, Stanislav. *The Adventure of Self Discovery*. Albany: State University of New York Press, 1988.

Jones, Alex. *Seven Mansions of Color*. Marina Del Ray: DeVorss & Company, 1982.

McKenna, Terence. *Food of the Gods: The Search for the Original Tree of Knowledge*. New York: Bantam Books, 1992.

Murphy, Michael. *The Future of the Body: Explorations into the Further Evolution of Human Nature*. New York: P. Torcher/ Perigee, 1993.

Ozaniec, Naomi. *The Chakras*. Rockport: Element Inc., 1990.

Zizek, Slavoj. *Looking Awry: An Introduction to Jacques Lacan Through Popular Culture*. Cambridge: The MIT Press, 1991.

Zizek, Slavoj. *Enjoy Your Symptom! Jacques Lacan in Hollywood and Out*. New York: Routledge, 1992.

OVER

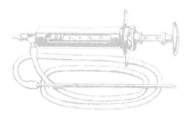

Characters

MANN and OTTER are brother and sister. They dress as if they were about to attend a high-end cocktail party.

Set

There are two chairs sitting side-by-side facing the audience. Between the chairs, there is a cord hanging from the grid which, when pulled, activates the lights.

Production History

Over was first produced in 1993 by Mammalian Diving Reflex and featured Darren O'Donnell as Mann and Veronika Hurnik as Otter, with direction by Darren O'Donnell.

Over was then produced in 1994 by Mammalian Diving Reflex, again with Darren O'Donnell and Veronika Hurnik, with direction by Daniel MacIvor.

Over was also produced in 1995 by Mammalian Diving Reflex with Darren O'Donnell and Veronika Hurnik, with direction by Karen Hines.

Scene 1

(Otter sits on the couch. Mann sits reading a dictionary in the easy chair.)

OTTER: *(shouting to no one in particular)* This man is a liar!

MANN: Oh, for Christ –

OTTER: This man is a liar!

MANN: Shut up!

OTTER: This man is a liar!

MANN: Shut up!

OTTER: This man is a liar!

MANN: SHUT! UP!

OTTER: You shut me up!

MANN: *(shouting to no one in particular)* This woman is a liar, this woman is a liar, this woman is a liar, this woman is a liar, this woman is a liar!

(Otter has a brief but violent temper tantrum.)

MANN: Are you happy now?

OTTER: I've got this feeling.

MANN: Uh huh?

OTTER: Just a feeling as to where all this is going to go.

MANN: Yeah, so?

OTTER: So, I want you to know that I know where this is going and, for your sake, I better tell you it goes no place nice for you.

MANN: Because of this feeling?

OTTER: I won't elaborate.

MANN: You can't elaborate.

OTTER: Okay, I can't elaborate. How can you elaborate on a fait accompli? You can't. It's a fait accompli.

MANN: I understand, you're angry.

OTTER: Just be careful what you say.

MANN: Look, listen, I understand.

OTTER: Yeah.

MANN: No really, I do.

OTTER: Sure.

MANN: You're angry.

OTTER: Yep.

MANN: You're very angry.

OTTER: Thank you for noticing.

MANN: You're irate.

OTTER: Yes.

MANN: You're so irate –

OTTER: Uh huh.

MANN: – that you've mistaken me for you.

(pause)

OTTER: This man is a liar!

MANN: Oh yes, indeed, Truth speaks!

OTTER: This man is a liar!

MANN: Right, you are if you say you are.

OTTER: This man is a liar!

MANN: Don't call you, we'll call us.

OTTER: This man is a liar!

MANN: *(loses his cool completely)* I HAVE A HEADACHE!

(Otter sharply points her finger at Mann. Mann covers his mouth in surprise. Otter snaps out the light. Blackout.)

Scene 2

(Otter snaps on the light and the scene is picked up midstream.)

OTTER: Oh Christ, listen to you, you maniac. You fucking maniac.

MANN: Listen to me? Listen to you! I can't make sense of any of this twisted dribble that leaks out of your fetid mouth.

OTTER: You're psychotic.

MANN: That's not my problem.

OTTER: No, you have no problems.

MANN: No, no I don't, I only have you. And that, my friend, makes any mere problem look like a vacation in the tropics.

OTTER: What do you know about the tropics? A soul as frozen as yours shrinks from even the word 'tropics'.

MANN: Tropics! Tropics! Tropics! I bask in the glory of that word 'tropics'. I suck in the humid air of your decaying soul and make it live and breathe!

OTTER: I can't make sense of you any more.

MANN: Anything anybody says about hopes and dreams and investments for the future, these things, these statements, these are, and I can't stress it enough, they are not promises. Do you hear me? They are not promises.

OTTER: Tell me another big fat lie.

MANN: I never promised you anything.

OTTER: You promised me the world.

MANN: And I gave you that.

OTTER: You promised me the moon.

MANN: That I couldn't confirm.

OTTER: You promised me hope.

MANN: I never promised that. That I could never promise.

OTTER: You prick. You worm. You can say whatever you want, but you know. You can believe whatever you want, but you know. You can believe you promised me whatever you want to believe and you may never have promised me hope but you certainly never promised me despair and that's all that's left, fucker.

MANN: LOOK, C'MERE, YOU CRIMINAL, YOU MERE CHILD MOLESTER, I'LL TWIST YOUR CUNT SO HARD, KNOT IT UP SO TIGHT, THAT WHEN YOU COME, AND YOU WILL COME, YOUR EYES'LL POP OUT OF YOUR FUCKING SKULL, DO YOU HEAR ME?!!

(Otter points her finger at Mann, while Mann covers his mouth in surprise. Otter snaps out the light. Blackout.)

Scene 3

(Otter turns on the light while Mann sits oblivious, reading the dictionary.)

OTTER: I had a dream.

(Mann says nothing, continues to read.)

OTTER: A man and a woman met on the coldest night of the year. They had been total strangers. He had gotten drunk and plopped his pants and she found him lying in the doorway of her walk-up apartment. She dragged him up two flights of stairs, the plop dropping down his pant legs. She undressed him, bathed him, washed his clothes, tucked him into her bed. She went to sleep on the couch and awoke to find him lying on top of her, his P inside her V. In the morning he held her in his arms and rocked her back and forth singing a song about John Henry, the railroad worker who'd had the race with the machine to tunnel through a mountain, who'd beat the machine only to step out into the sunlight and drop dead. And then I awoke and I was the one living in a walk-up apartment, I was the one washing his clothes, I was the one on the couch, I was the one tunnelling through the mountain, and I was the one dropping dead. And then I awoke.

(pause)

MANN: *(looks up, alarmed, as if he has heard a burglar)* Did you say something?

OTTER: We should move.

MANN: And live where?

OTTER: I wouldn't mind trying a walk-up apartment.

MANN: If you think you have a hard time sleeping here, I'd like to see you in a walk-up. You see, there is something cheap and sleazy about a walk-up, something about the odours of other people's food that waft down the hall, something about the illicit sex that seems to occur in every room of a walk-up. You get single mothers on welfare with no education, white-trash babies playing the sort of doctor that involves sticks and pointed pencils and a tight clothes peg on the sensitive spot. The cries of the underfed, undereducated, underloved children and the blood of the battered wives cake your every waking moment. The claw of death that descends on your soul in the middle of a bleak February afternoon when all the televisions are tuned to a soap opera, that claw will be the claw that scrapes on your inner eyelids every night your spongy head nestles into your greasy pillow. A sense of rape lingers on the mouths of everyone. Don't talk to me about walk-ups!

OTTER: Since when were you such an expert on walk-ups?

MANN: The walk-up is something I've spent many an hour contemplating.

OTTER: Apparently.

MANN: No, you just listen.

OTTER: I'm listening. How could I not listen?

MANN: Listen to me.

OTTER: I'm listening.

MANN: No, you're not, you're talking.

OTTER: I'm talking to tell you I'm listening.

MANN: You can't talk, tell and listen at the same time.

OTTER: I can.

MANN: Don't start up.

OTTER: Talk to me about walk-ups.

MANN: You better start counting down your days.

OTTER: Walk-ups.

MANN: Because it's not going to be long ...

OTTER: Walk-ups.

MANN: ... with this attitude of yours.

OTTER: Walk. Ups.

(pause)

MANN: The walk-up –

OTTER: *(cutting him off)* Yes.

MANN: You were an anemic child, you know.

OTTER: Yes, I know.

MANN: You don't have a lot of friends.

OTTER: I noticed.

MANN: You're more interesting than outgoing.

OTTER: Yes, I've always found you much more outgoing.

MANN: People take advantage of this weakness of spirit of yours.

OTTER: Do they?

MANN: Yes.

OTTER: I hadn't noticed.

MANN: My point exactly. Because I –

OTTER: Because you ... protect me.

MANN: Exactly. I protect you from a certain number of harsh realities which I often have to shoulder myself. The strain is enormous. I field abuse and torment that's intended for you and often come through a little the worse for wear.

OTTER: I'm sorry.

MANN: Completely my decision.

OTTER: Thank you.

MANN: Not at all.

OTTER: So why do you spend so much time thinking about walk-ups?

MANN: I was not a child of love. I was a child of rage. The kind of rage that a walk-up embodies. I will tell you this story only to stop you from fantasizing about walk-ups. It I will tell you for your own good. But also know that this story may cause you some pain. Do you have a complete understanding?

OTTER: Completely.

MANN: On the coldest night of the year, many years ago, before she had met Father, Mother returned home from work to her walk-up apartment to find him lying drunk on the front steps, steeped in his own excrement. She dragged him up two flights of stairs, the stool rolling quietly down his pant legs to softly bounce down step by step. She bathed him, laundered his clothing. By hand. Then tucked him into her bed while she made a nest of it on the couch. And after all that kindness she awoke to find him forcing himself on her. He remained on her until I was conceived in that most putrid act. How and why they remained together until their untimely deaths is another story, but suffice it to say, from that day forward, my knowledge of walk-ups is entirely extensive.

(Otter has fallen asleep on the couch. Mann hesitates, then moves to her and begins to stroke her hair. He pauses, then plugs her nose. She gasps for breath, reaches blindly out, and turns off the light.)

Scene 4

(Otter turns on the light. Mann sits for a moment in a daze.)

MANN: I had a terrific headache this morning.

OTTER: 'Terrific'? It was a good headache?

MANN: No, 'terrific', as in 'terrifying'.

OTTER: So, a bad headache.

MANN: Terrific headache.

OTTER: This sounds familiar.

MANN: It should.

OTTER: Of course, the time we debated 'fantastic'.

MANN: Yes.

OTTER: I still think a fantastic headache sounds like a good thing.

MANN: It wasn't.

OTTER: No, I guess not, and neither is a terrific headache, I suppose.

MANN: Not this one. I thought I was dying.

OTTER: Do you want a pill?

MANN: I feel fine now.

(pause)

OTTER: Mann?

MANN: What?

OTTER: What if it was an 'awesome' headache?

MANN: What?

OTTER: What if the headache was 'awesome'? Would that make it better?

MANN: If it inspired awe?

OTTER: Yes.

MANN: If a headache inspired awe then, sure, I'd say that would make it better.

OTTER: You thought you might die from this headache this morning?

MANN: It was like an anvil through the cranium.

OTTER: And you were afraid.

MANN: I was on the floor clutching my brains screaming.

OTTER: *(alarmed)* Where was I?

MANN: I don't know, I'm not a spy.

OTTER: You thought perhaps this was it. It was over, over, all over.

MANN: *(in amazement)* My thought exactly!

OTTER: That day is going to arrive for real, you know –

MANN: Yes.

OTTER: A once-in-a-lifetime experience –

MANN: Uh-huh?

OTTER: And you're going to whine your way through the whole thing.

MANN: If I hadn't promised Mom, I'd kill you right now!

OTTER: And I'd be AWESTRUCK! And that's the difference between you and me. Whiner!

(Otter snaps out the light.)

Scene 5

(Otter sits poised for action while Mann sits in a daze, the dictionary open upon his lap.)

OTTER: Mann.

(Mann doesn't respond.)

OTTER: Mann!

(Mann still doesn't respond.)

OTTER: MANN!

MANN: OTTER!

OTTER: *(alarmed)* What!?

MANN: Jesus Christ, Otter, I'm saying to you, 'Jesus Christ'.

OTTER: Why, why are you saying this to me?

MANN: *(rattles off the following text at a fevered pitch and speed)* Jesus Christ, Otter, life has dealt me blows that are inconceivable. I can't stress this enough. I sit here, ostensibly alone, I sit in the vacuum of this home, do you hear me, just sitting waiting for a better day. Not wholly confident that a better day will come but in fact totally convinced that the days are as good as they get. You can't blow into the wind with an attitude like this. You can't look yourself in the eye in the mirror in the morning on the eve of a new day with a goddamn attitude like this. You can't move. You goddamn can't move, you can't, you just can't.

OTTER: Mann.

MANN: Of course this is something we all have to deal with in order to grow –

OTTER: Mann.

MANN: – to change –

OTTER: Mann.

MANN: – to transmute.

OTTER: Mann.

MANN: Otter, what?!

OTTER: *(suddenly stands)* I'm a-movin' out.

(Mann is stunned, then snaps out the light.)

Scene 6

(Their positions have not changed from the previous scene as Mann snaps on the light.)

MANN: You, my little sister, are insane, do you hear me? Totally and irrevocably insane. There are factors of stress which I attribute some of this reaction to but, overall, entirely, there seems to be little rhyme or reason to this unabashed insanity.

OTTER: You're right, there's nothing. There's nothing. Nothing.

MANN: I don't know if you know the gravity.

OTTER: No, there's no gravity.

MANN: No gravity? You are a fool, a fool. I pick up this book and I let it go *(he drops the dictionary)* and what happens? Otter, I pick up this book and I let it go *(he drops the dictionary)* and what happens? Otter, I pick up this book and I let it go *(he drops the dictionary)* and what happens is : it falls. It falls and falls and falls. And that *(lets the book go)* is gravity. Now, I pick up this chair. And I let the chair go and what happens? Otter, tell me what happens.

OTTER: You are a liar.

MANN: That's wrong, you're wrong there. The answer is, simply, the chair falls. You see, I'll demonstrate more. You see, I am an object that lies in gravity's path. You throw myself into the air and what happens? *(he leaps into the air and comes crashing down)* You see? Gravity. No gravity? No gravity? Do you see how I've proved you wrong. I've totally taken you apart and left you standing there holding an empty egg.

OTTER: I was an anemic child.

MANN: *(confused)* Yes, you were.

OTTER: I have suffered.

MANN: We all have.

OTTER: Who do you think suffered the most?

MANN: Suffering is not, suffering is not, suffering has nothing to do with any of this.

OTTER: You have suffered.

MANN: Yes, I have.

OTTER: Mom suffered.

MANN: Absolutely.

OTTER: Dad suffered in his way.

MANN: Suffering is epidemic.

OTTER: Every day I scrub my hands. I scrub and I scrub and I scrub!

MANN: *(further confused)* No, you don't.

OTTER: I lie in bed, scrubbing my hands, I make breakfast and I'm scrubbing my hands. I try to read a book and I can't concentrate. I scrub. It's all I can do.

MANN: *(surprised)* I have a headache.

OTTER: Look how clean my hands are. Look at my hands!

MANN: I can see your hands clearly.

OTTER: See how clean they are?!

MANN: I see, I see!

OTTER: They're clean because I scrub. I scrub and I scrub and I scrub!

MANN: I hear you, I hear you!

OTTER: I can't stop scrubbing!

MANN: So don't, don't stop scrubbing!

OTTER: *(urgently)* I've read they're proving things.

MANN: *(even further confused)* Who's proving things?!

OTTER: Scientists. Philosophers. Psychologists.

MANN: But they're always proving things.

OTTER: They're proving things they shouldn't be proving.

MANN: Shouldn't? If they proved it, what does it matter? If it's proved it was always there to be proved, whether they proved it or not.

OTTER: That's exactly what they're not proving.

(Otter snaps out the light.)

Scene 7

(Whereas the previous scene was panicked, this short scene is relaxed and philosophical. Otter turns on the light.)

OTTER: They're proving things they shouldn't be proving.

MANN: Shouldn't? If they proved it, what does it matter? If it's proved it was always there to be proved, whether they proved it or not.

OTTER: That's exactly what they're not proving.

(Otter snaps off the light.)

Scene 8

(Mann snaps on the light.)

OTTER: My bags are packed.

MANN: So, pack your bags, girl. Pack your goddamn bags. You damn pack them. Pack them! Pack them! Pack your goddamn bags. Do you hear me? Pack them! Pack your goddamn bags. Pack them. Pack. Pack. Packpackpackpackpackpackpackpackpack packpackpackpack.

OTTER: I –

MANN: It's not about leaving, it's about packing. And you can pack your goddamn christless bags. You pack those bags, honey. You pack those bags, baby. You pack those bags good. You pack and you pack and you pack. You pack till your little heart's content. You pack and you pack and you pack. Do you hear me? Go ahead and pack.

OTTER: I'm already packed.

(pause)

MANN: Then you better unpack, sister.

OTTER: Is it because you'll miss me?

MANN: What?

OTTER: Is it because you'll miss me?

MANN: I might be ... lonely.

OTTER: With no one to talk at.

MANN: At?! ... At?! ... At?! ... At?! ... At?! ... At?! ...

OTTER: All right, Mr Mann, I'll ... STAY!

(Otter snaps off the light. This blackout is longer than the rest, signifying a shift in the play.)

Musical Interlude

Scene 9

(Otter turns on the light. She pauses, listening. Mann, oblivious, continues to read the dictionary.)

OTTER: Doesn't the buzz of the refrigerator bother you?

MANN: What?

OTTER: Buzz, buzz, buzz, all day long.

MANN: 'Buzz, buzz, buzz, all day long'?

OTTER: Buzzaporoids. Buzzulo. Buzzoinkidity-doink …

MANN: What?

OTTER: Buzza buzza buzza buzza buzza buzza buzza. Buzza buzza buzza buzza buzza buzza buzza. Does it? Does it bug ya? Does it bug ya?

MANN: *(earnestly)* I'm sorry, what is your problem?

OTTER: Problem? Schmoblem.

MANN: So … no problem.

OTTER: Not unless you have a problem with the perpetual, never-ending buzzing buzzing buzzing of the refrigerator.

MANN: What's wrong with the refrigerator now, for Christ's sake?

OTTER: Nothing that a brain transplant couldn't fix.

MANN: Oh yeah. *(resumes reading)*

(pause)

MANN: *(looks up from the dictionary, noticing something for the first time, tries to locate source, can't find it)* What is that Jesus noise?

OTTER: What noise?

MANN: I don't know, it's, um, it sounds like it's coming from outside.

OTTER: *(earnestly)* Outside of your head?

MANN: Outside of the house.

OTTER: Outside of the house?!

MANN: It's nothing, a mild whining sound!

OTTER: A puppy?

MANN: No, it's distinctly electrical in nature.

OTTER: The streetcleaner.

MANN: Smaller.

OTTER: A Rotorooter.

MANN: Those goddamn things are manual.

OTTER: An electric Rotorooter.

MANN: No.

OTTER: An electric whippersnipper, an electric blender, an electric blanket, an electric handgun pointed at your big fat pustulent –

MANN: I think it's that goddamn refrigerator.

OTTER: Which refrigerator?

MANN: Our goddamn refrigerator.

OTTER: You put our goddamn refrigerator outside?!

MANN: No, I didn't!

OTTER: Well, I didn't.

MANN: What are you talking about? The refrigerator is not outside, it's in the kitchen, where it belongs!

OTTER: Then what in the Holy Jesus name of Christ is whining outside?!

MANN: Nothing! I misheard. My ears are faulty. Forgive me. Or no, maybe … um … do you hear anything?

OTTER: I hear you clearly.

MANN: Do you hear this whining sound?

OTTER: 'This' whining sound? Which whining sound? I hear any number of whining sounds.

MANN: It's a particular one I'm after.

OTTER: A whining sound.

MANN: Yeah.

OTTER: A whining and dining sound?

MANN: No, just a whining sound.

OTTER: I hear the whining of a distant dog.

MANN: That dog's always whining.

OTTER: And I can always hear it.

MANN: This is something new.

OTTER: And unusual.

MANN: Yes. There's the whining of a distant dog –

OTTER: And then there's the buzzing of the refrigerator.

MANN: It IS the refrigerator!! It's loud! Goddamn refrigerator. It's
annoying. It's got me on the edge of my seat.

OTTER: Unplug it.

MANN: Could, could do that.

OTTER: The peanut butter would be easier to spread.

MANN: I'll take that into account.

OTTER: And that's all that's in there.

MANN: And ice.

OTTER: Ice in the freezer and peanut butter below in the fridge proper. And that's all that's in there.

MANN: I saw two packs of garlic and a clove of ketchup in one of the two drawers.

OTTER: All that buzzing for ice, peanut butter, two packs of garlic and a clove of ketchup, because that's all that's in there … unplug it.

(Mann hesitates. Leaves. Re-enters. Sits.)

MANN: Done. *(resumes reading, looks up)* I can still hear it.

OTTER: It's just winding down.

MANN: That's not how fridges work.

OTTER: How would you know?

MANN: No, there's something else.

OTTER: Maybe it's your pacemaker.

MANN: *(checks his head)* My pacemaker's fine.

OTTER: Are you sure it's outside of your head?

MANN: I think I know the difference between an imagined sound and a real one.

OTTER: That's not what I meant.

MANN: *(using his finger to emphasize his point)* Outside my head, inside my head. I know the difference. I know reality when I see it.

OTTER: Maybe your ears are ringing from listening to yourself talk.

MANN: Wait a minute.

OTTER: What?

MANN: My ears are ringing! It's discordant as hell.

OTTER: Maybe you're out of tune.

MANN: This could grow to torment me.

OTTER: Try to enjoy it!

MANN: How?!

OTTER: Hum along.

MANN: The melody's not clear.

OTTER: Hum the harmony!

MANN: Otter!

OTTER: Hum the harmony!

MANN: Otter!

OTTER: Hum the harmony!

MANN: Otter!

OTTER: I'm right here.

MANN: The ringing in my ears.

OTTER: What of it?

MANN: It's … it's … it's … professional.

OTTER: Professional?

MANN: Professional! It sounds like a choir. There's a church in my head! It sounds like there's a church in my head, there's a church in my head! Oh my God!! Oh my God!! A church has gotten into my fucking head! There's a church in my head! Help! Help! Help!

OTTER: MANN!!

MANN: I can't concentrate! I can't think! This noise! This harmony! This church! This choir! This Beethoven!

OTTER: Beethoven?!

MANN: It's Beethoven!

OTTER: Ludwig Van?

MANN: Yes!! Oh yes!! Ludwig Van! Ludwig Van!

OTTER: You look like you're liking it!

MANN: *(starting to cry)* I'm loving it! Oh my God, I'm loving it!

OTTER: *(pulls the dictionary out of Mann's hands)* Well, can you love it a little quieter? I'm trying to read a book.

MANN: I'M HEARING BEETHOVEN!

(The dictionary leaps out of Otter's hands.)

OTTER: What the – !

MANN: It stopped.

OTTER: Your goddamn book jumped clear out of my hands.

MANN: It's not mine, it's the library's.

OTTER: Ownership aside, for God's sake, it leapt like a catamaran out of my paws.

MANN: Of its own volition?

OTTER: I have every reason to suspect so.

MANN: At the exact same moment Beethoven stopped playing.

OTTER: Beethoven, the music, or the man?

MANN: The music. *(with amazement)* Maybe the man!

OTTER: Beethoven, he himself?!

MANN: Could've been, could've been. Was the music, could've been the man, but frankly what's leaving me perplexed … is this book.

OTTER: It seemed to pulse and then leap.

MANN: It pulsed.

OTTER: Then leapt.

MANN: Like a monkey.

OTTER: Exactly like a monkey.

MANN: Funky.

OTTER: What?

MANN: Funky.

OTTER: Funky?!

MANN: I said 'funky'.

OTTER: I heard the word, I just missed the gist.

MANN: Oh, then I'll explain. I'd call such an occurrence 'funky'.

OTTER: Funky.

MANN: As in 'leaving me in a funk'.

OTTER: You're in a funk.

MANN: I feel funked by the whole thing.

OTTER: Are you sure your use of the word 'funk' is correct?

MANN: Look it up.

OTTER: *(goes to the book with caution, picks it up, opens it, then becomes frightened)* I opened the book to the very page.

MANN: *(even more frightened)* Mere coincidence.

OTTER: 'Funk: a state of paralyzed fear, panic.'

MANN: *(becomes utterly relaxed)* That about describes me.

OTTER: You look relaxed.

MANN: Don't judge a book by its cover.

OTTER: Or by its pulsing cover.

MANN: Either. *(which he pronounces 'I-ther')*

OTTER: Either. *(which she pronounces 'E-ther')*

MANN: You see, I know something's wrong, I just don't know what.

OTTER: Coincidentally, I'm feeling the same way.

(pause)

OTTER: *(growing quietly alarmed)* Hey.

MANN: What?

OTTER: I just peed my pants a little.

MANN: It's called … incontinence.

OTTER: I'm not incontinent! I'm too young!

(pause)

MANN: *(growing alarmed)* Hey.

OTTER: What?

MANN: I just peed my pants a little too.

OTTER: I'm told it's called … incontinence.

(They sit confused for a moment, then together tentatively turn out the light.)

Scene 10

(This scene is a dream which is occurring to both. The dialogue is very fast and vaudeville-like with a great many takes to the audience. Each line is accompanied by a choreographed gesture. Xylophone music plays. The light, a nice moody blue spot, turns on seemingly by itself.)

OTTER: The sky is wonderful.

MANN: My hands are hot.

OTTER: We could go down to the lake and you could dip them in.

MANN: I'd rather shove them in a bucket of ice, frankly.

OTTER: The refrigerator's unplugged!

MANN: S'pose I could just … run them under the tap.

OTTER: Is your mouth dry?

MANN: Now that you mention it.

OTTER: Could I afford to kiss it?

MANN: That's between you and the bank.

OTTER: I'm looking for a second opinion.

MANN: I wouldn't call myself an expert.

OTTER: So don't.

MANN: Okay, I won't.

(Otter leaps into Mann's arms.)

OTTER: Suck it!

MANN: What the –

OTTER: I just said suck it!

MANN: Well, I just don't understand.

OTTER: *(with pity)* Oh, Mann.

MANN: Isn't it about time for that kiss?

OTTER: I think it just might be.

MANN: Lay it on me. *(Otter jumps to the ground)* Sister.

(They kiss like fish.)

OTTER: If this isn't heaven –

MANN: I don't know what is.

BOTH: And if this isn't hell … THEN NOTHING IS !!!!!

(They kiss like fish.)

OTTER: Do you remember 'Nude Statues'?

MANN: *(confused)* Nude Statues?

OTTER: Nude Statues.

MANN: No. No thanks. No Nude Statues, whatever the hell that is, for me. Thanks – *(Otter leaps into Mann's arms)* goodnight.

OTTER: Mann, you might get a grip once in a while.

MANN: You better hope my grip is fine or I'll drop you.

OTTER: All four feet.

MANN: You could break a wrist.

OTTER: I'll risk it, Mr Mann.

MANN: I'm a-gettin' tired.

OTTER: How 'bout that kiss?

MANN: How 'bout it, it was good.

OTTER: How 'bout another one?

MANN: How 'bout?

OTTER: What's holding you back?

MANN: Propriety?!

OTTER: What took you so long?

MANN: Look, listen – *(Otter jumps to the ground)* you kiss me fair and square.

OTTER: And that about does it.

(They kiss like fish.)

OTTER: Mom used to wax her bikini line in front of me before we'd go down to the beach.

MANN: Oh?

OTTER: Yes, she'd spread her legs.

MANN: Really.

OTTER: Then she'd smear the hot yellow wax onto her coarse inner thighs, all the while screeching and squirming.

MANN: I'm finding this hard to swallow.

OTTER: So did I. When it had dried she'd pull it off with a snap while Douglas the Dog howled and yowled.

MANN: Grotesque!

OTTER: Then she'd toss the hardened hairy wax to Douglas who would busy himself chewing it for the rest of the afternoon.

MANN: Yeeesh!

OTTER: Yeeesh indeed.

(Otter reaches up slowly and pulls an imaginary light cord and the lights snap to black.)

Scene 11

(The light snaps on by itself.)

MANN: WHAT THE?

OTTER: MANN!

MANN: Otter, for Christ's sake!

OTTER: *(stutteringly confused)* I, I, I, I …

MANN: Mother had no pubic uncertainty!

OTTER: She did! She did she did she did she did she did!!

(pause)

BOTH: What?

OTTER: I think I might have been dreaming.

MANN: That's funny –

OTTER: You're not laughing.

MANN: – I too might have been dreaming.

OTTER: That is funny.

MANN: You're not laughing either.

OTTER: Just give me a couple of minutes.

MANN: Take your time.

(pause)

OTTER: Do you remember Nude Statues?

MANN: Nude Statues!

OTTER: Nude Statues.

MANN: Nude Statues.

OTTER: WHAT WAS YOUR GODDAMN DREAM?!

MANN: *(stunned into remembering a vague snippet of the dream)*
    I dreamt –

OTTER: Uh huh.

MANN: I dreamt …

OTTER: What did you dream?

MANN: Uh … uh …

OTTER: THINK!

MANN: I don't know … it's vague.

OTTER: I think you're vague.

MANN: I know I'm vague, but frankly so is the dream.

OTTER: Think!

MANN: Okay! Okay! Okay! *(he drops the panic completely)* Why the panic?

OTTER: *(she too drops the panic)* I don't know. *(resumes the panic)* Just think!

MANN: I am thinking!

OTTER: Assume a fetal position.

MANN: Otter, I haven't assumed a fetal position since I was born.

OTTER: Why don't I assume a fetal position?

MANN: Otter, do whatever the hell you like.

(Otter lies in a fetal position.)

MANN: Oh yes. I dreamt. Yes, it's … *(horrified by the thought)* oh my God!

OTTER: What?

MANN: I actually dreamt of a land without consequence.

OTTER: You'll have to be a little more specific.

MANN: A land totally lacking in consequence. No consequence. None.

OTTER: What is this no consequence?

MANN: I dreamt.

OTTER: Uh-huh.

MANN: Of a land.

OTTER: Yes?

MANN: Of a land.

OTTER: Of no consequence.

MANN: Of this land where there were no consequences … at all … for any given … action … or no, because, no, there just weren't any consequences … for anything.

OTTER: So what could possibly happen in this land?

MANN: *(utterly confused)* Nothing, *(in horror)* except I took you in my arms.

OTTER: You took me in your arms?

MANN: I took you in my arms.

OTTER: Which would ... what? Ordinarily have grave consequences.

MANN: *(confused by the word)* Ordinarily?

OTTER: Ordinarily.

MANN: Ordinarily?

OTTER: Ordinarily, in a land fraught with consequence.

MANN: What's this ordinarily talk?

OTTER: You know, ordinarily.

MANN: Ordinarily what?

OTTER: So you took me in your arms.

MANN: Yes. The end. I took you in my arms. The end.

OTTER: And that was the whole dream.

MANN: That was the dream, take it or leave it.

OTTER: Where would I take it?

MANN: THEN LEAVE IT!

OTTER: Should we try it?

MANN: What are you getting at?

OTTER: Just to test this land of ordinary consequences.

MANN: I know how the consequences work in this ordinary land.

OTTER: *(quietly)* Ordinarily.

MANN: What?

OTTER: Nothing.

MANN: I know how the consequences work here.

OTTER: Do you want an award?

MANN: I said I know how consequences work here.

OTTER: And I said I might be able to fashion you an award out of a piece of ... say, cardboard and glue.

MANN: You didn't say that.

OTTER: No I didn't, I said 'ordinarily'.

MANN: Okay. Fine. And what did you mean?

OTTER: Figure it out.

MANN: I'm not going to take this any further.

OTTER: So don't.

MANN: Okay. I won't.

(pause)

MANN: *(growing fear)* Is there something out of the ordinary here?

OTTER: Are you asking me?

MANN: Aren't you the only person here?

OTTER: I might be.

MANN: Might?! What's this might?

OTTER: I have a sneaking suspicion.

MANN: Yes?

OTTER: When you took me in your arms.

MANN: Uh huh.

OTTER: In the dream.

MANN: Yes.

OTTER: Well …

MANN: Yes.

OTTER: Um …

MANN: Yes!

(Otter inhales as if to speak but stops.)

MANN: WHAT?

OTTER: Well … I had a dream.

MANN: So?

OTTER: So.

MANN: So, what?

OTTER: So, that's what happened in my dream.

MANN: I took you in my arms?

OTTER: The very same.

MANN: Yiipes!

OTTER: And –

MANN: More?!

OTTER: There were others there.

MANN: OTHERS?

OTTER: *(looking very pointedly at audience)* Like there are now.

(They sit sort of staring out at the audience for a long time.)

OTTER: Mann.

MANN: Otter?

OTTER: Try to relax.

MANN: Relax?

OTTER: Let them look at you.

MANN: Them? Do you really consider Them a them?

OTTER: You're right, they're more an It.

MANN: But a big IT!

OTTER: A ubiquitous IT.

MANN: An everywhere IT!

OTTER: Only more so.

MANN: More than everywhere.

OTTER: It's all!

MANN: It judges.

OTTER: Harshly.

MANN: It's punitive!

OTTER: It can be nasty.

MANN: Terrible!

OTTER: It can be lovely!

MANN: Beautiful.

OTTER: Horrible.

MANN: Lovely.

OTTER: Terrible.

MANN: Beautiful, beautiful, beautiful!!

BOTH: It feels like …

OTTER: It feels like … *(in terror, her mouth wide open … tries to say the word but has a hard time getting it out)* US.

MANN: Yes, it's us. It's us. It's us.

OTTER: Only –

MANN: Yes?

OTTER: More so.

MANN: More so?

OTTER: More so than us.

MANN: I really need to turn off the light now.

OTTER: Allow me.

(Otter turns it off with a scrunch of her face. Mann gasps.)

(in the blackness)

OTTER: Mann?

MANN: Otter?

OTTER: I think we can be both here and there.

MANN: Here and there?

OTTER: Here and there: two places at once.

MANN: We can?

(pause)

OTTER: Mann.

MANN: Otter.

OTTER: You should coin a new word.

MANN: A new word?

OTTER: For being here and there: two places at once.

MANN: Uh … uh … what about … 'applejack?'

OTTER: Mann, with a word like 'applejack' this ability of ours will be just another tree paved over by history.

MANN: My feeling?

OTTER: Yes?

MANN: Pave away.

OTTER: Here and there.

MANN: Otter, please.

OTTER: Here and there.

MANN: Don't.

OTTER: Here and there.

MANN: *(surprised by the inspiration)* Over!

OTTER: Over?

MANN: Over.

OTTER: Over. It's good, I like it. Where are you?

MANN: Over.

OTTER: Seems to work. I'm over myself. I've gone from a state of being here or there to a state of being, quite frankly, everywhere.

MANN: We're everywhere?

OTTER: We're over.

Epilogue

(The two stand amongst the audience observing the stars with awe. A twirling glitter ball illuminates the room.)

OTTER: Oh my – !

MANN: The sky is wonderful.

OTTER: *(pointing to the heavens)* That's Panopticon.

MANN: Panopticon. Hm.

(pause)

MANN: *(pointing at a falling star)* Did you see that?

OTTER: Yeah.

MANN: Gorgeous.

OTTER: *(pointing)* It looks like the birth of a black hole.

MANN: One can only hope.

OTTER: I once knew a dancer named Hope.

MANN: Do you remember Nude Statues?

OTTER: Like the back of my hand.

MANN: *(pointing)* Whoa! Did you see that one? I'll bet it hit the ground.

OTTER: *(feels for a moment)* No, it didn't.

MANN: Are you over?

OTTER: A little.

MANN: I'm just Here.

OTTER: *(pointing at a spectacular shooting star)* Whoa!

(The two freeze and hold their positions for about ten seconds. Lights fade to black.)

End

Acknowledgements

I would like to acknowledge the support and encouragement of Sky Gilbert, Naomi Campbell and Libby Zeleke. The support of the Toronto Arts Council, Ontario Arts Council, Canada Council and the Laidlaw Foundation was also crucial to these plays.

In the case of *White Mice*, I would like to acknowledge Tanisha Sri Bhaggiyadatta, who strongly influenced my understanding of the situation, and Bruce Hunter, who provided dramaturgical advice.

About the Author

DARREN O'DONNELL is a playwright, director, actor, occasional set designer and the artistic director of Mammalian Diving Reflex. His writing credits include *Boxhead*, *pppeeeaaaccceee*, *White Mice*, *Who Shot Jacques Lacan?*, *Radio Rooster Says That's Bad*, *Recent Developments in Biotechnology* and *Mercy!* He is also the co-creator of '2 See Love', a music video for the band LAL. Darren is currently working on his first novel, *Your Secrets Sleep with Me*, and his first short film, *Dying Days*.

Darren was the 2000 recipient of the Pauline McGibbon Award for his directorial work, the 2000 recipient of a Gabriel Award in broadcasting for his CBC radio piece *Like a Fox*, received Dora nominations for outstanding play, direction and production for *White Mice* and won for his and Naomi Campbell's set design. Darren has twice been nominated for the John Hirsch Award for young directors.

Typeset in Sabon
at Coach House Printing on bpNichol Lane, 2001

Edited and designed by Darren Wershler-Henry
Copy edited and proofread by Alana Wilcox
Photographs for *White Mice* by John Lauener
Photographs for *Who Shot Jacques Lacan?*, *Radio Rooster Says
    That's Bad* and *Over* by Aarin MacKay

To read the online version of this text and other titles from
Coach House Books, visit our website:
www.chbooks.com

To add your name to our e-mailing list, write:
mail@chbooks.com

Toll-free:
1 800 376 6360

Coach House Books
401 Huron Street (rear) on bpNichol Lane
Toronto, Ontario
M5S 2G5